AL SMITH

AMERICAN

By FRANK GRAHAM

AL SMITH
AMERICAN

AN INFORMAL BIOGRAPHY

By FRANK GRAHAM

G · P · PUTNAM'S SONS

NEW YORK

Manufactured in the United States of America

VAN REES PRESS · NEW YORK

The author is deeply grateful to members of the Smith family and to the many friends of the late Governor for the aid they so generously gave in the preparation of this book. He also wishes to thank the Museum of the City of New York for the use of the pictures which they placed at his disposal.

CONTENTS

ILLUSTRATIONS

AL SMITH

AMERICAN

1: A BOY RUNNING IN THE STREETS

THE BROOKLYN BRIDGE WAS NEW, AND THE
people of the East Side not only used it as a means for
getting to Brooklyn but on bright days it was their prome-
nade, and on summer nights when the moon was high, young
couples strolled, arm in arm, back and forth across the span.
Great sailing ships from all the ports of the world were
moored at the East River docks, unloading their cargoes of
fruit and coffee and spices and tea, and so close did they
crowd the edge of the city that their bowsprits made a line
of spears over the South Street cobbles. Drays, drawn by
stout horses, hauled away the treasures the ships had brought,
and there were chandleries along South Street and sailors'
boardinghouses in all the streets near by.

Small boys played along the water front, scampering about
the ships, playing hide and seek among the crates and bales
that cluttered the docks, swimming in the river when summer came, building snow forts when the winter drifts were
piled high. They hung about the doors of the firehouse in
John Street, where Engine 32 had its quarters, talking with
the firemen, petting the horses, and waiting with but thin
patience for an alarm to ring that they might race down the
street behind the engine, mingling their cries with the shrill
blasts of its whistle and the vibrant clang of its bell.

They lived in the tenements or the molding old private
houses on James Street . . . and Oliver and Water and Dover
. . . and all the streets that huddle about the Bridge. They
were, for the most part, the sons or grandsons of Irish im-
migrants who had found new homes within walking distance

3

of the berths of the ships that had brought them to this country. Their fathers were dockmen or truck drivers or laborers or worked in the Fulton Fish Market and struggled desperately hard to give their children the opportunities which they themselves never had enjoyed.

The children, although sometimes keenly aware of the seriousness of the battle for existence being waged by their parents, were happy in their games and their sports and the bustling, exciting life going on all about them. They never had known . . . and most of them never would know . . . the rippling brook, the forest, the sight of cows grazing in a pasture or wheat fields stirred by a summer breeze. They never had trudged, barefooted, along a dusty road nor tickled trout nor plucked apples from a tree or watermelon from a vine. But who could have wished a better playground than theirs? The streets . . . the river that rolled by, almost at their doorsteps . . . the towering ships back from voyages to Europe and South America and China and India and all the far places of the world . . . the market, fairly bulging with fish hauled from the deep waters of the Atlantic . . . the firehouse . . . the Bridge that arched not only over their homes but over their lives as well.

There was among them, in that time, one who was destined for greatness, whose name would be known across the face of the earth. He would be famous for his integrity, his thoughtfulness, his kindliness, his charity, and his breadth of vision. He would be respected, honored, even idolized by his decent fellow Americans—and vilified by the mean, the vicious, and the ignorant. He would be elected governor of the great state of New York four times and would be denied the presidency of the United States only after a campaign which is remembered chiefly because of the courage with which he marked it. His life would be an inspiration to the youth of the nation, and at his death the nation would sorrow.

But now he was quite indistinguishable from the other small boys whose world was a corner of the island of Man-

The South Street Al Smith Knew As a Boy

Al Smith's Mother

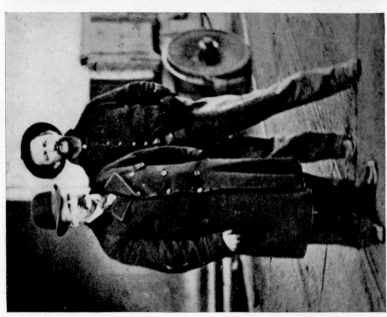

Al Smith's Father (right) and a Friend

hattan. He played on the docks, swam in the river, walked on the Bridge, mingled with the dock wallopers and the bronzed and tattooed sailors home from the sea, chased the fire engines, and attended St. James's Parochial School at the corner of James Street and New Bowery. His clothes were as poor as the others', his face and hands as dirty after a romp in the streets, his marks in school no better or no worse than the average. His light hair and gray eyes, his bright countenance and ready laugh, didn't set him apart from a dozen other boys. If he could claim any distinction whatever, it was that he could yell louder than any of his companions.

His name was Alfred Emanuel Smith.

All that was long ago and . . . as it must have seemed to him in later years . . . far away. The house in which he was born has been torn down and the site is occupied by a gas station and small parking lot. Another house in which he lived is gone, too; and most of the others . . . for he lived in many houses . . . are on the wreckers' list. The Downtown Tammany Club, which was his political cradle, is a crumbling hollow shell, its windows boarded up, its insides charred by a fire that, ironically, broke out on an election day when the voters of the district were sending a Republican to the Assembly.

St. James's School still echoes to the shouts and murmurs of children. Across the street, the church where he was baptized and where he worshiped for years has taken on the color of age, which has enhanced the dark beauty of its interior, but time has scarred its outer walls, and the auditorium in the basement, where he once trod the boards, has been demolished. Gone are the graceful sailing ships from the South Street water front and in their places are freighters with stumpy masts and funnels. The firehouse has disappeared from John Street. Only the Bridge looms, unchanged, against the sky.

There is, curiously, but one outward sign that he was born in these surroundings and, from there, went on to greatness. This is a card on a pew in St. James's, which he and his family occupied. And yet in the old houses and on the corners of the old streets they still talk of him almost as if he had left Oliver Street only yesterday. Father Keane at St. James's . . . Robbie Weisberger, who has a shoe store on the corner of Catherine and Madison and whose father made shoes for his father . . . Tom Coleman . . . Jack Perry . . . Charlie Naples, whose saloon is at Catherine and South . . . Tony Vanella, the undertaker . . . Nick Walsh, the real estate man on Pearl Street . . . Mamie Collins, sweet-faced, white-haired, still living at 9 Oliver . . . the Gleasons and the Gillespies and the Martins and the O'Flahertys, the Palumbos and the Gardellas and the Ginsbergs and the Cohens.

There are the churlish among them, of course. Forgetful of the way in which they imposed on him, they remember only the favors they asked of him that he couldn't grant and hold these denials against him. Some still are resentful that, in the prime of his political life, he left the old neighborhood and went uptown to live among the swells. But most speak of him with a feeling that borders on reverence, remembering all he did for them and all like them who, needing a break, got it only because they constantly were in his thoughts.

The Second Class in St. James' School with Al Smith the Second from the Left in the First Row

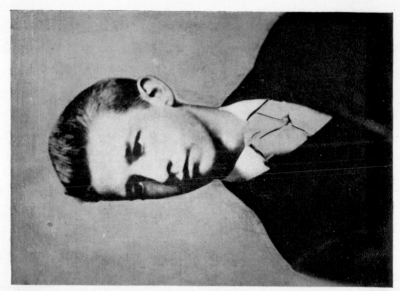

When He Was Nineteen Years Old

When He Was Four Years Old

2: CHILDHOOD AND BEREAVEMENT

AL SMITH'S MATERNAL GRANDPARENTS, Thomas and Maria Mulvehill, came to this country with their infant son, Peter, from Westmeath, in Ireland, in 1841. A clipper ship of the Black Ball Line, which had brought them across the sea, docked at the foot of Beekman Street, and with the child and their scanty luggage they set out on foot to find a home in the new land. They had gone but a few blocks when, at the corner of Dover and Water Streets, they saw a sign:

"Rooms to let."

It was a neat house that bore the sign.

"We'll stop here," Thomas said.

The house was owned by a grocer named Dammerman, whose store occupied the first floor. The Mulvehills took the second floor, put the baby to bed, and settled their few belongings. They had, in all truth, found a home. It was there that their daughter, Catherine, was born and from there that, in September of 1872, she was married to Alfred Emanuel Smith, a boss truckman whose stable was next door to the Dammerman house.

Smith was fifteen years older than Catherine and a widower with one daughter. He was a tall and powerful man, with a long, weather-beaten face and a heavy, drooping mustache. He was born on Oliver Street between South and Water and was a well-known figure in the neighborhood, and had some local fame as a waterman, being a skillful boatman and an expert swimmer. A good storyteller and popular in the truckyards, the corner saloons, the chandleries, and along

7

the water front; and yet, for some reason, little or nothing was known about him or his people, for he never talked about them or where they came from.

Having sent his growing daughter to live with relatives in Brooklyn, he set up housekeeping with his bride at 174 South Street. This was a four-story house, with a store on the ground floor. On December 30, 1873, a son was born to the young couple.

"He shall be called for you," Catherine said. "Alfred Emanuel Smith."

Al was two years old to the day when his sister was born. She was called Mary.

It was about this time that the Smiths had an opportunity to buy a farm.

"The boss wants me to take it," Alfred, Sr., said, telling his wife of the offer when he came home from work one night. "He says we can pay for it at the rate we're paying rent here."

The rent was fifteen dollars a month.

Mrs. Smith's eyes lighted.

"It would be fine," she said. "It would be a good place for the children to grow up."

Her husband shook his head.

"No," he said. "I thought about that and I'd like it for them. But there are too many other things to think about. We've always lived in the city and I don't know whether we'd be happy there or not. And who'd run it, with me working the hours I do—and as hard as I do? I've got to be near my job, and I get little enough rest and I don't want to spend my Sundays farming. No, it won't do."

"Where is the farm?" his wife asked.

"In South Brooklyn," he said. "It's too far out. Even Harlem would be better than that. There are good farms up there, too, if a man wanted one. But not as cheap as this one."

He shook his head again.

"Aw!" he said. "I wasn't meant to be a farmer."

His wife was silent. If they could run the farm it would be different. Or if it could be made to pay, so that they could hire somebody to run it for them. But her husband had his trucking business—he worked, under contract, for a machinery firm and it was the junior member of the firm who had offered him his chance to move to the country— and it would be folly to sacrifice that to take up farming, of which neither of them knew anything. And, as Alfred said, he couldn't manage both the trucks and the farm at the same time.

Thus the decision was made. But the story lingered, and Mrs. Smith was to tell it to the children many times in after years.

"That was our chance to get rich," she would say with a smile.

The farm in South Brooklyn was in the region of Fifth Avenue and Fifty-fifth Street which, in years to come, would leap a hundredfold in value as sites for apartment houses.

Young Al and his sister played on the South Street sidewalk in front of their home or watched, fascinated, the building of the Bridge, the New York tower of which had been completed in the year that Alfred was born. Now workmen fashioned the great span, which cut across the sky directly above their home, and swung into place the great cables that supported it. Memorable was the day on which it was opened. It was May 24, 1883, and the occasion was marked by a parade by day and fireworks by night—and by a lively protest from the Irish societies, strong throughout the city, because May 24 was Queen Victoria's birthday.

Even more memorable in the lives of the children was the tragedy six days later when, with the Bridge thronged by Memorial Day sightseers, someone cried that it was about to fall and panic swept the crowd. Al and his sister and some of their playmates, startled by faint cries of alarm from the dark roadway above them, looked up to see hats, coats, pocketbooks, and parasols raining to the cobbles. Soon the near-by streets were filled with clanging fire engines, police patrol wagons, and ambulances, and Al and some of the other boys, running to the Park Row approach to the Bridge, were horrified to see the victims of the crush being rushed to the hospitals—or the morgue.

The Smith children were baptized by Father Felix Farrelly of St. James's Roman Catholic Church on James Street, between Madison and New Bowery, which already was old, having been dedicated in 1837, and which today is the oldest Catholic church in New York housed in its original structure, although there are three older parishes in the city. In 1880, when he was seven years old, Al entered the parochial school, diagonally across the street from the church, on the corner of New Bowery. One day he was to claim, laughingly, the Fulton Fish Market as his alma mater. Actually, this was it. His formal education was limited to the eight years he spent at St. James's, and the record he left behind him there gave no hint of the future in store for him. By all accounts he was a well-mannered boy, not given much to the fist fighting that sometimes marked the recesses or that period directly after school when the children, released from the classrooms for the day, tumbled into the street, yelling, laughing, pushing, jostling each other—or squaring off in combat. He was popular with the Christian Brothers who taught him, but he was far from being a star pupil.

"I never was much of a scholar at St. James's," he was to say in after life. "The only creditable record I made was that I was seldom absent and never late. And I couldn't even claim the credit for that. My mother saw to it that, rain or shine, I went to school every day unless I was sick, and she also saw to it that I got there on time."

There were many other places that were more attractive to him than the classroom—the streets, the docks, the river, the Bridge, above all the firehouse on John Street. All the boys naturally gravitated to the fire house, but none as regularly as he. His lifelong devotion to the Fire Department and the excitement which he always found in chasing the engines and watching the firemen at work was born in those long-gone days. He never achieved his first ambition—to emulate his uncle, Peter Mulvehill, who drove Hook and Ladder 10 on Fulton Street, and wear the blue shirt of the New York Fire Department—but in that respect his frustration was not complete: there would be a day when his friends in the Department would confer upon him the rank of Honorary Deputy Chief.

But that day was far distant when he practically haunted the quarters of Engine 32. He ran errands for the firemen, helped them to polish the bright work on the apparatus, and carried coffee and sandwiches to them when they fought fires on bitterly cold days and nights.

It was in 1881, in Al's first year in school, that Father John J. Kean succeeded Father Farrelly as pastor of St. James's. The change was not altogether popular at first. Father Farrelly was beloved by all the parishioners, and they were a little in awe of the new pastor whose reputation as an administrator and an orator was city wide. Used to the plain, easygoing ways of Father Farrelly, they were uneasy, in the beginning, in the presence of this tall, dark, handsome newcomer; but he soon won their love and confidence, and his interest, not only in their spiritual welfare but in their recreation and their ordinary day-to-day lives, had a tremendous influence on them. Not the least affected by his coming was Al Smith.

Father Kean may be said to have been the first man to guide the footsteps of the boy. In his mother he found a source of inspiration not only in his childhood but through all the days of her life; but his relations with his father were limited by circumstances. He loved his father and was loved by him in turn. He was proud of his father's strength, the way he cleft the waters of the river with powerful strokes or rowed a boat against the strong tide. There were occasional excursions with his father to Coney Island or up the river to one of the groves that dotted the Harlem shore, and there were visits with his father and mother and sister to one of the beer gardens along the Bowery, where he sat enraptured by the music of German bands or listened to his father's stories and, now and then, was allowed a sip of his father's beer.

But the elder Smith worked long hours, and when he came home at night he frequently was so tired that he went to bed soon after supper—no one ever referred to the evening meal as dinner—and there would be days and nights on end when Al saw so little of his father that there was small chance of a real companionship growing up between them. Looking back, in later life, he confessed that he knew little of his father save that he was a hard-working man, sober, kindly, and devoted to his wife and children. Of all the stories he had heard from his father, he could remember none that had to do with his father's early life. They were, instead, stories of the trucks and the horses and the water front, of swimming races and boat races and pleasure trips up the river and down the bay.

Father Kean, looking in at the children in their class-rooms, wandering among them while they were at play in the streets, was attracted to this light-haired, loud-voiced boy who, although certainly no scholar and in no way superior to his companions in any of the games they played—he had, for instance, no use for baseball or boxing and could not run or swim any better than the others—seemed somehow to be a dominant figure among them.

"There," he thought, "is one worth watching."

He had to admit, even to himself, that he didn't know what it was that set Al apart from the rest of the boys, but somehow there was an appealing quality about him. Maybe it was his poise, for never, even as a small boy, did Al lack for assurance.

Al was ten years old when Father Kean asked him if he would like to serve on the altar at St. James's. The priest was pleased when he said he would.

The news that he had been selected as an altar boy was received with joy by his mother.

"Perhaps," she said to her husband, "he will grow up to be a priest. Wouldn't that be wonderful?"

"It would," her husband said, "but I doubt that he will."

He was right. Al always would be strong in his faith and would defend, in dramatic circumstances one day, his inherent American right to worship as he chose. But, as his father knew, the boy had no great fondness for books, religious or otherwise, and showed no inclination to study for the priesthood or, for that matter, anything else. The serious application which was to make him, in time, one of the best-informed men in America had not yet been developed within him, nor would it be for many years. Nor, devout as he always would be, would he ever yearn to wear the habiliments of the church.

He served faithfully as an altar boy. Even in the winter months, when the boys drew straws to see who would serve at six o'clock mass, he did not complain that, as almost invariably happened, he drew a short straw. Unforgettable with him but never to be regretted were the bleak cold mornings he trudged up Cherry Hill to the church past the darkened houses that lined the way.

In 1884 the little family moved to 316 Pearl Street, having been forced to vacate their rooms on South Street because the building had been sold. And now tragedy was drawing slowly but relentlessly about them. In 1885 the father's health, broken by years of hard work, with few vacations and little relaxation of any kind, compelled him to seek a less arduous way of making a living. He sold his horses and trucks, but horses were cheap and trucks were, too, and the meager proceeds of the sale soon were spent for doctors and medicine. Unable to do manual labor and unfitted for skilled employment, he took the only job open to him, that of a night watchman.

The rent at Pearl Street, little though it was, was too much for them and in the spring of 1886 they moved once more, this time to 12 Dover Street. It was there that, in November, the father died. Al and his mother and sister were quite penniless, but friends rallied about them in their sorrow and need and saw to it that the funeral expenses were paid.

Now a grim battle for sustenance loomed ahead of the mother and her two young ones—Al was not quite thirteen and Mary not quite eleven. Mrs. Smith could have appealed to charity, of course, but she was not gaited this way. This was to be her battle and she would fight it her way. By her own efforts she would keep the little home together until Al was old enough to help her. Even then he wanted to quit school and go to work, but she would not hear of it.

"You must have more education," she said. "You are a fine, brave boy, but for a time, anyway, I can manage."

There was not a day to be lost. And so, after supper on their return from the cemetery, she set out with Al to see the forewoman of an umbrella factory where she had worked for a short time before her marriage. It was arranged that she should return to the factory on the morrow and that, to supplement her earnings there by day, she should take work home with her at night.

And so the fight was launched by this frail but determined woman. It was a bitter one, and Al never would forget a moment of it: his mother rising early to get breakfast for them, and preparing the lunches they carried. Seeing them off to school and then going to work. Coming home at night, getting supper with Mary's aid, and then, after the supper dishes had been cleared away, bending over the work she had brought home with her. And somehow finding time to keep their little flat clean, and washing and mending the children's clothes.

But it couldn't go on. Not that way. After a year, the mother's health was affected. Another year...or less...and she would have broken down. And now the landlady of the Dover Street house came to her assistance. There was a store in the basement of the house that had been vacant for some time.

"Why don't you take it?" the landlady asked. "All the fixtures are in good condition. All you need is some stock."

"What kind of stock?"

"Oh, candy...groceries...something like that. You are well known in the neighborhood. I am sure you would make a success of it. And while it wouldn't be easy work, it would be easier than the work you're doing now."

Mrs. Smith shook her head in despair.

"Where would I get the money to stock the store?" she asked. "I have nothing."

The landlady smiled.

"That's where I come in," she said. "I will lend you the money and you can pay me back when the store is a success."

Mrs. Smith talked it over with Al, who, for all his youth, had developed within the year of sharp adversity a mature way of thinking. He was very much in favor of it.

"Sure, Mother!" he said. "Let's do it. Mary and I can help you run the store. We'll get along fine."

And so the vacant store was cleaned and stocked with candies and dry groceries and opened for business. Trade was fairly steady, and although it was obvious from the beginning that the store would be no bonanza, it afforded a means of existence. Most important, it greatly lessened the physical strain imposed on the mother. And to pad the family income, however slightly, Al set up a little business of his own, taking over a newspaper route in the neighborhood. Mary helped her mother in the store while Al delivered his papers after school. In the evenings he was in charge in the store and his mother, with no more home work to do, could sew or read one of the newspapers he had brought home, or go to bed early.

For a year they managed fairly well, but more money was needed to maintain even their modest home than the receipts from the store and Al's earnings as a newsboy. And so, a month before he would have been graduated from St. James's, Al left school and went to work as a chaser for William J. Redmond, who operated a fleet of trucks along the water front. His job was to pick up trucks wherever they might be and deliver orders to the drivers, thus saving time that would be lost if, having discharged a load, a driver had to return to the office to find out where he must go next.

The job required a complete knowledge of the lower East Side, with emphasis on the market districts; and fleetness of foot and soundness of wind. Al had all three, thanks to his early training gained in running about the streets and the docks. The pay was three dollars a week—little enough to compensate him for not having received a diploma at St. James's—but it represented an increase over the returns from his newspaper route. Besides, he thought the job was fun. He now was being paid for racing up and down South Street and the streets that jutted from it, skipping nimbly through the heavy horse-drawn traffic, pausing to rest, now and then, on one of the docks or at one of the market stalls —all of which he had been doing for nothing for seven or eight years.

But whether he realized it or not, he had put his childhood behind him. Henceforth he was not only to earn his own living but to be, increasingly, the chief support of his mother and sister—to be, in every sense of the word, the man of the house. It isn't likely that his break with school caused him a very deep regret. He never had cared much for school, anyway, save for one phase of it. That was the class in elocution, of which he was one of the foremost pupils. Indeed, he already had won a couple of medals in debating contests with other schools. For the rest—for the down-to-earth reading, writing, arithmetic, history, and geography—he had never given off any signs of enthusiasm. A passing mark in any subject was all he ever desired—and all he ever achieved.

3: THE FULTON FISH MARKET

THE TRUCK-CHASING JOB LASTED TWO YEARS. In 1890 he left it to go to work as office boy and assistant to the shipping clerk in the oil firm of Clarkson and Ford, which was on Front Street near South. This meant a jump of five dollars a week in salary, and Al, now in his seventeenth year, regarded himself as quite the young man.

He wore long trousers and a narrow-brimmed brown derby hat. He was experimenting with the smoking of cigars and the drinking of beer. He went to dances and began to take an active interest in the dramatic society of St. James's, which gave its performances in the auditorium in the basement of the church. As a pupil in the school he had been an enthusiastic patron of the drama as it was portrayed by the boys and girls of the school and was smitten by the beauty and acting skill of Mamie Leary, who was the belle of Oliver Street and the female lead in all the shows. She was four years older than Al and, of course, regarded him with no more interest than she did any of the other little boys in the school. But it is probable that she, more than any other, had sharpened his interest in the society. Now he was a member of it, and in the near future would become the star of its productions, playing heroes and villains with equal vigor and putting his strident voice to excellent use as he vowed to save the heroine, when he was the hero, or to have her, and curse you, Jack Dalton! if he was the villain.

It was, he thought—and he was right—an exciting era in which to be approaching manhood, especially if you lived

THE FULTON FISH MARKET

on the lower East Side of New York. There was n
for anyone to journey far from that section in quest
when the day's work was done. There were fine ho
lower Broadway and the best actors on the American stage
appeared at the Windsor or People's Theatre on the Bowery
or the Academy of Music on Fourteenth Street. There were
dance halls and music halls and museums on the Bowery,
and lantern-lit restaurants in Chinatown. There were social
clubs, such as the Seymour Club, founded by Henry Campbell, who lived on Catherine Street and kept a wholesale
grocery on Vesey Street. A wealthy bachelor, he gave much
of his time and money to the club, of which Al and most
of his friends were members.

There were church excursions up the East River or the
Hudson in the summer, and the outings of the numerous
political clubs. There were torchlight parades at election
time. There were prize fights and ball games, although Al
himself cared nothing for these sports, and bicycle trips to
Brooklyn or the far reaches of Harlem or the Bronx, which
he enjoyed very much. There were parades of ragamuffins on
Thanksgiving Day and fancy dress balls at Arlington Hall.
When snow and ice covered the city's streets—and in those
days no one ever thought of clearing the streets after a storm
—there would be long sliding ponds on South Street and
tobogganing on Dover Street or any other street that sloped
toward the river.

In two years he rose to a junior clerkship in the oil company office, but his pay remained eight dollars a week. It
was imperative that he earn more than that, for expenses
were mounting at home and trade had fallen off so badly
at the store that there was now but a thin trickle of small
change across the counter. He knew that it would not be
long before their business venture would have to be closed
out and written off, and so he looked about for a job that
would put more than eight dollars in his weekly envelope.

It was at the suggestion of one of his friends that he

went to work in a place that always will be associated with his name: the Fulton Fish Market. His employer was John Feeney and he was called—or liked to call himself—assistant bookkeeper, which probably meant that he scratched receipts and expenditures in an account book when the boss was busy. Actually, he helped to roll in—or out—barrels of fish, put the fish on ice, clean them, sell them, and wrap them. It was hard, rough work and the hours were long—from four o'clock in the morning to four in the afternoon, except on Fridays. On Fridays he started work at three o'clock in the morning. But the pay was good—twelve dollars a week—and each night he was permitted to take home as much fish as he would.

The four extra dollars a week and the saving in food costs made possible by the free fish were tremendously important at home, and the store was abandoned. Of course, the regularity with which fish appeared on the table became monotonous after a while, but at least it was good, fresh fish and it didn't cost anything, although it did lead to a recurrent and frightening dream for at least one member of the family.

"I used to dream that a big fish was pursuing me, with his jaws wide open," Al once said. "It seemed he wanted revenge for all his relatives I had eaten."

After nearly four years in the fish market, he crossed the Bridge to Brooklyn for a new job at another hike in wages, going to work as a shipping clerk for the Davison Steam Pump works. The hours were shorter and the tasks assigned to him not too hard, and it is altogether possible that if the pump works had been nearer home, he might have remained there. But the journey back and forth palled on him after a while and once more he looked about for a change of employment.

When he found it—or, rather, when it figuratively was dropped in his lap—it changed the course of his life. He had become mildly interested in politics, and now, through the good offices of his friend Henry Campbell, he received an appointment in the office of former Judge Thomas Allison, the Commissioner of Jurors. He was designated as a clerk, but his assignment was that of a server of summonses to jury duty. This took him all over the city, including the Bronx, which then was a part of New York County, and while he quickly discovered that tapping a businessman for jury duty did not make him precisely popular, he enjoyed the new glimpses of the town that he was getting now. He also enjoyed—for he looked upon it as a sort of game—tracking down those who sought to elude him, or outwitting them when they tried, on one pretext or another, to get free of him when he had caught up with them.

He liked, too, the little prestige he gained from going to work for the county. Moving about, going into the fine hotels, the exclusive clubs, and the homes of the wealthy— and the humble gathering places or abodes of the poor—a far more important figure than a toiler in the fish market or a shipping clerk in the pump works. He wore his hat at a more rakish angle, frequently paid a dime instead of a nickel for his cigars, and in every way became more of the man in that new world that was opening itself to him.

4: ROMANCE ... THE DRAMA ... AND MARRIAGE

MEANWHILE, LOVE HAD MOVED INTO HIS LIFE and dealt him a terrific blow in the heart. He knew when he first saw her that she was the only girl in the world for him. He knew it with a fierce certainty that drove him to overcome the obstacles that lay between them and to win her at last. And he was right, for through all the rest of his life he loved her devotedly, as she loved him, and when she died it was not long before he followed her.

Her name was Catherine Dunn and she was pretty and witty and charming and good. She, too, had been born in the Fourth Ward, but when she was very young her family moved to 170th Street and Third Avenue, away up in the Bronx. It could have been, since they so obviously were destined for each other, that they would have met on one of the occasions that, as was her custom, she visited the home of her uncle, who was a policeman and lived on Catherine Street. But as it happened, they were brought together by her cousin, Johnny Heavyside, the policeman's son. There were, it appears, some papers to be signed that had to do with the family plot in Calvary Cemetery, and Catherine's mother's signature was needed, so Johnny was dispatched to the Bronx. Since it was a long journey by elevated railroad and trolley car, what more natural than that Johnny, wanting company, should ask his friend Al to make the trip with him—and what more natural than that Al and Catherine, being two very nice young persons, should be attracted to each other? At any rate, that's the way it happened, and it wasn't long before Al regularly was sacrificing hours of

A Bathing Party at Coney Island in the Nineties

Mr. and Mrs. Smith with Alfred, Jr. and Emily

needed sleep after a long day in quest of prospective jurors so that he might see the girl with whom, from the very beginning, he was so very much in love.

Between visits to the Bronx—the seriousness of which Catherine's father and mother did not realize at first—he was seeing plays from the galleries of the Bowery theaters and applying the lessons learned there in his appearances with the St. James Players. Rapidly becoming the star of the cast, he soon had virtually a choice of roles. He liked the villains' parts best, since they were fatter.

"All the hero has to do," he boasted, "is to throw out his chest and win the girl. It takes an actor to be the villain."

It is doubtful that he ever had any ambition to become a professional actor, but since he was acting for fun, he wanted to get the most fun out of it. That, he felt, he could get by playing the best roles up to the hilt, and that's the way he played them. In fact there is a story still going around in the old neighborhood that he was such a convincing villain the school kids hissed him whenever he passed by. And that this made such an impression on him he thereafter wanted naught but to be the hero.

The St. James Players didn't have to go back to antiquated playbooks for amateurs to find vehicles for their talents. Their skill was so widely recognized among actors and managers and producers who had seen them perform, and the worthiness of the group was so appreciated—the receipts from the shows helped largely to maintain an orphanage conducted by St. James's—that the right to reproduce even plays that were running currently on Broadway or the Bowery was freely granted to them.

Al played the Honorable Bardwell Slote in *The Mighty Dollar* as nearly as he could like William J. Florence, a popular leading man of the day, whom he had seen at the Thalia; Jem Dalton in *The Ticket-of-Leave Man;* Alfred Huntington in *All the Comforts of Home,* a role in which William Faversham and William Gillette had appeared;

Alexis Petrovich in *The Russian Honeymoon;* and Arthur Carringford in *Hazel Kirke.* His greatest success, however, was scored as Corry Kinchela, the villain, in Dion Boucicault's *The Shaughraun.* He received such excellent notices for this in the newspaper columns devoted to amateur theatricals, then very popular in New York, that some of his friends spread a rumor that his services were being sought by a number of Broadway producers.

Serving summonses by day . . . acting . . . going to the theater or courting Catherine Dunn by night . . . growing into manhood . . . widening his acquaintance . . . being watched, covertly, by the politicians, always on the lookout for young men of poise and promise, young men who were liked by their neighbors and, in time, might do the party some good. And, all the time, working hard to get ahead, to make more money, to prove to Mr. and Mrs. Dunn in every way he could that he was worthy of their daughter—or as worthy as anybody could be.

He still hadn't asked their permission to marry her, and therefore was not formally engaged to her. But not being altogether unobservant, they were becoming aware of his deepening interest in Catherine and noted, with some uneasiness, her deepening interest in him. Uneasiness? Well, he was a nice young man, of course. Hard-working and decent and a good Catholic, and everybody they knew seemed to think so well of him but . . . well, they were afraid his prominence with the St. James Players might have given him serious ideas about turning to the professional stage. They liked the theater well enough, of course. But liking the theater was one thing and having your daughter marry an actor was another. Actors were all very well in their way, no doubt. Seen on the other side of the footlights, some of them were quite pleasing. But that was the place to keep them. On the other side of the footlights. Not in the family. Not marrying your daughter . . . and being out of work for weeks on end, perhaps, and, generally speaking, leading a strange and fanciful life in strange and fanciful surroundings. It wasn't to be the wife of an actor that they had raised Catherine and educated her well. Let her marry some serious businessman, who would provide a decent home for her.

Al, although sensing that his campaign for Catherine's hand wasn't going too well, save with Catherine herself, was unaware for some time of the nature of the objections which the Dunns harbored. When he learned of it, he quickly set their minds at rest. He had, he insisted, not the slightest desire to become an actor. He was eager to make a solid place for himself in the city, county, or state government. He already had won recognition from the Commissioner of Jurors and had been promoted from a process server to an investigator.

"It's something like a detective," Al explained. "When the regular process servers can't find the man they're looking for, they turn the case over to me."

And, with no little pride:

"I find him."

Well, it was good that he didn't want to be an actor. But how about the matter of supporting Catherine? She had been reared in a comfortable home, and, her parents being a little better off than those of most of the girls she knew and (ahem!) the young men, too, for that matter, she had enjoyed certain advantages of which they did not like to see her deprived.

"Don't worry about that," Al said. "If I didn't know I could give her a good home, I wouldn't ask her to marry me."

The Dunns were satisfied on all points. The last barrier had been broken down. And so, on May 6, 1900, Al and Catherine were married in the Church of St. Augustine on 167th Street between Fulton and Franklin Avenues in the Bronx. The ceremony was performed by Father Kean, who came all the way up from St. James's.

Al's mother now went to live with her daughter and her

husband, John Glynn, a policeman, who had moved to Brooklyn and were beginning to raise a sizable family. Al and Katie—as he called her then, and always would—had rented a small flat near the water in Bath Beach for the summer. When the reception following the wedding was over, they embarked on their wedding trip—by elevated and trolley car to Bath Beach.

In the fall the young couple naturally reverted to the old neighborhood, going to live at 83 Madison Street. There, on January 26, 1901, a son was born to them. He was called Alfred Emanuel Smith, Jr., and Al went about proudly distributing cigars to his friends.

5: ENTRANCE INTO POLITICS

LOOK AHEAD TWENTY-FIVE YEARS. AL SMITH IS the Governor of the State of New York and a young woman reporter is interviewing him in his office in the capitol at Albany. She is trying very hard to get from his own lips a story that will give a new slant to her readers on this man who has come from the sidewalks of New York's East Side to the position he now holds. With his aid she has explored his school days and has found therein no clue to his rise. She reasons there must be another guidepost. Perhaps it is to be found in his reading.

"Tell me," she asks, "what important books you have read."

By this time he is amused. He leans back in his chair, takes a cigar from his mouth and says:

"Young lady, the only book I ever read from cover to cover was *The Life and Battles of John L. Sullivan.*"

Bewildered by his reply but sticking gamely to her quest, she asks:

"What, then, is the secret of your political success?"

Now the Governor is serious. There is another puff on the cigar and then:

"Just being around."

Now cut back twenty-five years. It is 1901 and, in his own words, the future Governor is "just being around." He has moved from Number 83 Madison Street to Number 79, and he has joined the Downtown Tammany Club. He still is serving summonses for the Commissioner of Jurors and he has seen some of the small, inner workings of local politics

27

and is eager for some kind of political office himself. The Assembly, lower branch of the state legislature, is in his mind. He means, somehow, to get there some day. Most important, he has discovered, is to be around.

The one he had to impress with his quality as political timber was Tom Foley, whom he had known almost as long as he was conscious of having known anybody. Foley, big, quiet, hard-working, sincere, had just triumphed over Paddy Divver in a bitter battle for leadership, a battle in which Al had supported him by working as a district election captain, and now was the undisputed but benevolent boss of the lower East Side. Godfather to countless children of his henchmen, unfailing to the faithful in time of need—he would pay the rent, buy the coal and the groceries, bail out an errant son apprehended by the police, meet doctors' bills, and get jobs for those who wanted work—he demanded repayment in but one currency: a vote for the Democratic ticket, from top to bottom, in any election.

In a time when most political bosses were corrupt, Tom Foley was a shining exception. He was a saloonkeeper and a rough-and-tumble guy, but he was decent. He could—and did —make or break aspirants to public office within his domain, but he never asked one of them to do anything of which the aspirant could have reason to be ashamed. He began as a poor man and—although this is a long way ahead of the story —he died one. Had he been willing to traffic with some of the dive keepers who were eager for his support, he could have made a fortune, but he rebuffed them in angry disdain, and the moneys that came to him from legitimate sources trickled steadily through his hands into those of his constituents. Sometimes even all he had was not enough. He would be broke and somebody would go to him to borrow money, needing it desperately, and he would say:

"I haven't got it but I will get it for you."

And he would borrow it or arrange for the suppliant to borrow it, giving the lender his own promise that it would be repaid even if, in case of further misfortune for the borrower, he had to repay it himself.

Foley's headquarters was the Downtown Tammany Club, housed in an imposing brownstone building on Madison Street. He owned two saloons, one on the corner of James Slip and South Street and the other on Center Street, near the Criminal Courts building, and he spent some time each day in one or the other. But mostly, day or night, he could be found at the club. His constant presence there, and his personal attention to every detail of the political state of his bailiwick, made him the most powerful leader in the city, not even excepting Big Tim Sullivan, over on the Bowery. He was a good listener and spoke but seldom. When he spoke, you knew he spoke the truth, for he had a deep scorn for liars.

"Never make a promise unless you intend to keep it," he told the young men around him.

This was the man who could launch Al Smith on the political career he had dreamed up for himself—this man and this man only. And now Smith was "being around." When he had finished his day's work, he would go home and have supper with Katie and young Alfred—Emily, the first girl, was born that year—help Katie to clear away and wash and dry the dishes, and then he would be off on his rounds.

The first stop...and very often the last...would be the club. Foley would be there, of course, and some of the district captains, such as that likable young Italian who called himself Tony Kelly and who, because of his suave manner and debonair dress, was called "the Count" by his friends. There would be Joe O'Leary, who worked in the District Attorney's office, and other young fellows who, like Al himself, were politically ambitious and were eager to serve Foley as messengers or in any other capacity. Al would wait around, talking with the others, hoping Foley would have something for him to do. If there were no contracts—a favorite word with Foley—to be executed, he would leave after a while, dropping in at the Seymour Club, at McCaffrey's pool parlor at 36 Catherine Street, at some of the near-by saloons.

He would meet Tommy Christie, whose tenor voice already was making him mildly famous in the small-time vaudeville houses and beer halls. And Jack Gilchrist and Jack Cushion and Pat Whalen and Tom Campbell and the three Coleman boys. He never was much of a hand for standing at the bars but liked the back rooms, where, in most places, there was a piano. And he would sit around, drinking beer and joining in the songs as Johnny Heavyside or someone else thumped the piano.

He knew everybody—and everybody knew him: the decent people, who made up the bulk of the neighborhood's population . . . the gangsters such as Chick Tricker and Eat 'Em Up Jack McManus and Indian Louie, whom he would meet in the Bowery hot spots or on the fringes of Chinatown. He saw the inside of the political brawls that flared as an election approached. He was there one night when guns barked in one of those brawls at the corner just below the clubhouse and a man was killed. Yet he walked calmly, cleanly, through the rougher phases of the neighborhood politics, untouched and unperturbed by the violence that sometimes broke out all about him.

He had served two years of his apprenticeship when his chance came. In 1903 he was living at 9 Peck Slip and there was another baby in the household—the girl, Emily. The assemblyman representing the district was Joe Burke, handsome, personable, young, eloquent, and, Foley had thought when he first had sent him to Albany, promising. But Joe had found life too easy, too pleasant. His mounting popularity had stimulated him but not, Foley thought, in the right direction. His social engagements took up so much of his time that his absences from the club, at first sporadic, were becoming common. When Foley spoke to him about his lack of attention to his duties, he answered airily:

"Take it easy, Tom. Why should I have to spend all my time around here? You know where to find me when you want me."

Foley looked at him in silence for a moment, then walked away from him. Had Burke been a keener observer, he would have seen the smoldering anger in Foley's eyes and noted the sharp line into which his mouth had been drawn. But Joe's mind was on the pleasant evening he had planned for himself, and he was in high spirits, as usual, when he left the club a few minutes later. Foley, watching him go, made up his mind right there that if Burke ever returned to Albany it would not be as an assemblyman from his district.

An election was approaching. He went over in his mind the young men who were rising about him in the club, young men on whom he could depend and who, given the opportunity that Burke had tossed away so lightly, would apply themselves to it earnestly. His first choice was Pat Whalen, who was a clerk in the office of District Attorney William Travers Jerome. He called Pat into his office the next night.

"How would you like to go to the Assembly, Pat?" he asked.

Pat was startled.

"What's the matter with Joe Burke?" he asked.

Foley shook his head.

"Never mind Burke," he said. "I'm asking you if you want to go to Albany."

Pat thought it over for a moment.

"I'd rather go to the Board of Aldermen," he said.

"No," Foley said.

"Why not?"

"You're too young and don't know enough," the boss said bluntly. "Besides, I've promised that to somebody else."

Again Pat was silent. Then he asked:

"Can I talk to you about this tomorrow? It came as such a surprise to me I'd like to think it over."

"Go ahead," Foley said. "There's no real hurry about it,

although I'd like to know as soon as you make up your mind."

The following day Pat said to Jerome:

"Tom Foley wants to send me to the Assembly. Do you think I should go, Mr. Jerome?"

"No," Jerome said. "If you take my advice, you will stay where you are. There is no future in being an assemblyman. Look around and you'll see a lot of former assemblymen walking the streets looking for a job. From what you've said, I gather Joe Burke will be doing the same thing soon."

Pat nodded.

"I guess so," he said. "Anyway, I'm glad to hear you feel the same way about it that I do. I'll stay here until I can get a crack at the kind of job I want."

"Good," Jerome said. "Let Foley get somebody else."

That night Pat told Foley of his decision. The boss shrugged.

"All right," he said. "Have it your way."

Word that Burke's number was up got about quickly. Apparently the only one who didn't hear it was Burke himself. Forewarned of the blow that was about to fall on him, he might have averted it by pleading with Foley for another chance and then going back to work in earnest. Unaware of what was happening to him, he went his laughing way serenely.

One who had heard of Foley's decision was Henry Campbell. He went at once to the clubhouse.

"I hear Burke is through and you are looking for someone else to send to Albany," he said.

Foley smiled.

"News travels fast, doesn't it?" he asked.

"Is it true?"

"It is."

"Have you thought of Al Smith?"

"I have."

"Well?"

Foley looked at him thoughtfully. Then:

"Do you think he'd make a good man?"

"I do," Campbell said firmly. "I have known that young man almost all his life. Of all the young men in this neighborhood—and as you know, I have been as close to them as anyone and have tried as best I could to help those whom I thought deserving—he is the best and likeliest. He is hardworking, serious, and honest. His home life is exemplary. He is known—and liked—by everybody. Tom, I can't think of anyone better that you could pick for the Assembly."

Foley nodded.

"That's what I've been thinking," he said.

He didn't tell Campbell he had offered the nomination —and inevitable election—to Pat Whalen, nor did he tell anyone else. Having exacted a pledge of secrecy on that score from Pat, he knew the pledge would not be violated. Nor was it. Indeed, it is doubtful if Smith himself ever knew that he had been Foley's second choice.

Smith, summoned by Foley shortly after the boss's brief conference with Campbell, was elated at the offer made to him. He neither asked for nor needed time to think it over. His thoughts had been along that line constantly for two years.

"I'm very grateful to you, Tom," he said. "I'll always be grateful. And I'll do my best to be a credit to you when I get to Albany."

"I know you will," Foley said.

Then Al said, soberly:

"I'm so glad this opportunity has come to me. It means so much to us ... to Katie and me. And yet, I am sorry about Joe Burke. I don't like to feel that I am advancing at the expense of someone else."

Foley dismissed his qualms ... and Burke along with them ... with a wave of his hand.

"Never mind Burke," he said. "Don't feel sorry for him. He had his chance and threw it away. You act like he did and you won't go back to Albany, either. You do your job right and you can keep on going back as long as you like."

The next morning Al told Judge Allison that although it had not yet been made public, he had accepted the nomination to the Assembly. The Judge was not as pleased as Al had thought he would be.

"You are making a mistake," he said.

"A mistake!"

"Yes, Al," he said. And then, almost word for word, he repeated Jerome's warning to Pat Whalen: there was no future for a man in being an assemblyman unless he were a lawyer. All he had to do was to look about him and he would see any number of former assemblymen walking the streets looking for jobs.

Assemblymen obviously were not held in high esteem in those days. They were regarded, even by other politicians, as puppets of the bosses, allowed to remain in Albany only so long as they pleased the bosses, and subject to humiliation and removal at the bosses' will. Al Smith, the Judge thought, was too fine a young man to have his future jeopardized in a spot like that.

Al's confidence in himself, and in Foley's integrity, was not to be shaken even by the disapproval of a man whose opinions he valued.

"Don't worry about me," he said. "I am sure that if I perform my duties at Albany as I should, I won't be walking the streets looking for a job. All I will have to do is to keep thinking of the people who sent me there and do the best I can for them and I will be all right."

Katie shared his confidence in himself and his future as an assemblyman. Neither of them dared to look much farther ahead than the Assembly. That was enough to excite them and make them glad and grateful, for it proved that Al had demonstrated his worth to Foley. And yet they were sure, somehow, that fine things lay in store for them.

At the Assembly convention, held as a matter of form,

since Foley wanted Smith and that was all there was to it, so far as his subjects were concerned, Al received the nomination officially. In compliance with custom, he was not present during the voting. He was—and where else would he be? —at St. James's Union waiting to be notified. Two delegates called for him there and escorted him to the hall on Madison Street where the convention was held, and his heart leaped wildly at the applause that greeted his entrance.

Only one failed to join in the general acclaim at his nomination. This was Joe Burke, who, although he felt he had been shabbily treated by Foley, directed his anger not so much at the boss as at Al. The young men had been good friends up to that time, and Al was bewildered by Joe's hot words. His bewilderment swiftly gave way to deep resentment of Joe's attitude and the friendship was broken. It was not until many years later, when they met at the funeral of a friend, that they spoke to each other again.

Even the Divver crowd that had fought Foley so stubbornly could not quarrel with the choice of Smith as the party's nominee. The war between the factions was not over —sniping would go on for years, even though old Paddy Divver had died—but now a banner urging the election of Smith was stretched across the street in front of the Divver clubhouse, and the knowledge that at least he had effected a truce was a cause for added pride on Al's part.

Al campaigned briskly—and loudly—from the tail of a truck that was drawn through the distict, his brazen voice being heard clearly over the other noises of the streets. He was entered in a four-cornered fight, his opponents being a Republican, a Socialist, and a Prohibitionist. He had nothing to fear from any of them—least of all, in a neighborhood like that, from the Prohibitionist. He received 4,942 votes, while the Republican got 1,472, the Socialist 106, and the Prohibitionist, 5.

Al's mother and sister came over from Brooklyn on election day, and when the polls were closed and victory was certain, neighbors crowded into the little flat on Peck Slip for a celebration. Perhaps no other similar celebration he ever was to know would be as memorable, for this was the first. His cherished dream of being sent to Albany had been realized.

Two good friends were very helpful to him as an immediate aftermath of the election. Judge Allison, although disappointed perhaps that Al had not taken his advice and rejected the nomination, looked up the law on the subject covering the salaries of county officials elected to office and found nothing therein to prevent him from continuing to serve in the juror's office until he went to Albany on the first of the year, thus saving him the loss of nearly two months' salary. And Henry Campbell, having sponsored his candidacy, was determined that he would be dressed in a fashion to reflect credit on the district, and bought him a cutaway coat and a full dress suit at Brooks Brothers.

6: THE ARRIVAL OF BOSS MURPHY

THE ELECTION OF AL SMITH CREATED EX-
citement only in his district and even there the excitement was mild, since it had been a foregone conclusion from
the night of his nomination. Elsewhere in the city it went
unmarked. He was but one of many assemblymen elected or
re-elected, and if this elicited any comment beyond the boun-
daries of the district it was simply to the effect that Tom
Foley had broken one young officeholder—and made another.

There was, however, genuine interest throughout the city
in the rise of another, and, at the time, much greater political
figure: Charles Francis Murphy had become, in 1903, the
boss of Tammany Hall. His ascent had been both rapid and
unobtrusive. Few, other than those close to him, knew very
much about him, and even as time went on and his power
increased, the outsiders were to learn very little more. To
describe him as taciturn was to understate his remarkable
capacity for silence. It is doubtful if any political figure,
including Calvin Coolidge, ever used words as sparingly as
he, and in time there would be a standing line in the newspapers to cover his reaction to a request for his comment on
any given situation:

"Mr. Murphy said nothing."

Silently, then, he had hammered his way up through the
ranks, and now he was in absolute command of the fortunes
of Tammany Hall. These, because of friction among the
lesser leaders over a period of a year or so, were not as high
as they had been. Within a short time, working silently but
tirelessly, he was to repair the damage done by the squab-

blers. And now because he was to take a keen personal interest in Al Smith, and because his influence would enhance
the young man's steady advancement in office, it might be
well to pause and take stock of him.

Charlie Murphy was a product of the Gashouse district
which lies on the East Side in the Twenties. Like Smith, he
had had little formal education, but he had the same native
intelligence and the same solid determination to make something of himself. His first job was in a shipyard on the East
River front, and his first ambition was to excel in physical
prowess. To the hours of hard manual labor he put in every
day, he added hours of grueling training and constant practice in the sports most favored in that robust neighborhood.
Broad-shouldered, deep-chested, powerfully muscled, hard-
hitting, swift in all his movements, he was the best fighter,
the best baseball player, the best oarsman, the best swimmer,
and the fastest runner in that part of the city. He played with
a semiprofessional baseball team, won countless rowing, running, and swimming races, and was urged repeatedly by his
friends to become a prize fighter. To that urging he merely
smiled and shook his head. Whatever future he had planned
for himself, it did not include the prize ring.

He quit the shipyard to become a driver on the horse cars,
then quit the cars to open a saloon. It was in his saloon that
he first became interested in politics, which up to that time
had engaged his attention only on election days, when he
voted the straight Democratic ticket, of course. District captains and ward heelers were among the customers attracted
to his place by his reputation as an athlete, his quiet affa-
bility, and his propensity for setting up drinks on the house
with commendable frequency. Standing behind his bar or,
sometimes, standing in front of it sipping a glass of milk or
ginger ale—for he never drank or smoked or, for that matter,
even swore—he listened to their endless talk of politics. He
studied them closely, formed his own conclusions as to their
wisdom or the lack of it, assayed their influence on the voters,

and coldly appraised the value of the candidates they sponsored.

Now and then they asked for his opinion. He gave it simply, and noted with interest that they usually accepted it even when it did not conform with their own already expressed ideas. He noted, too, and with increasing interest, that when they took his advice, it almost invariably brought about the desired results. There came a day when he decided that there was no magic to the game of politics and that it might be played successfully by anyone with slightly more than average intelligence and a willingness to apply himself to it seriously. There was no reason, he thought, why he couldn't make a place for himself in the party councils, since he was smarter than most of his customers and had a stronger and more resolute character.

And so, quietly, he began fashioning his own district machine. Almost before they realized it, many of the neighborhood political workers were lining up with him, and in a short time he was a district captain. From there he moved up to become district leader, and now his influence, wielded from his club, the Anawanda, on Twentieth Street, was being felt at Tammany Hall on Fourteenth Street.

In January of 1902, Richard Croker, most powerful boss the Hall had had since the late, unlamented William Marcy Tweed, announced his virtual retirement—he didn't say positively—and sailed for Ireland, there to set himself up on an estate he had purchased with the proceeds of his leadership. Tammany had been under a heavy fire from the reformers, and this increased with the withdrawal of Croker. Wiser heads realized that, in order to forestall an even more intense attack, some degree of reformation must be accomplished within the Hall and, as a respectable front man, they elected Lewis Nixon, a brilliant young engineer of national reputation and unquestioned honesty, as leader. His tenure was of but a few months' duration. Gifted as he was in his own field, and interested as he was in the welfare of his party,

Nixon was not fitted for the post into which he had been thrust and was greatly relieved when his resignation was accepted.

Now the real battle for the peak began. Most vociferous of the aspirants for leadership was William S. Devery, who had been the last chief of the New York Police Department, the office having been abolished with his leaving. Now a real estate operator and a district leader, he tussled savagely for the top job and openly derided those who opposed him. When, marking time until they could settle on one man, the district leaders placed control of the Hall in the hands of a triumvirate consisting of Murphy, Daniel McMahon, and Louis F. Haffen. Devery sneeringly referred to their choices as "Sport," "Two Spot," and "Joke."

Smarting under the rough humor of Devery and the laughs it evoked through the city, the triumvirate failed to function properly. It was inevitable that one of the three would prove stronger than the others and establish sole control. It was inevitable, too, that this one would be Murphy, since he possessed qualities that the others lacked. By September he had demonstrated so clearly that he was best of the three that he was elected. There still was talk of the possibility of Croker's returning from Ireland to recapture the spot he had relinquished, but Murphy soon intrenched himself so firmly that such talk died away.

"Croker couldn't come back now if he wanted to," the Tammanyites said.

Under Murphy there were sharp changes in the conduct of the Hall. He gathered about him young, honest, serious men with whose characters and methods not even the reformers could quarrel. One of those was to be Al Smith.

7: "THE WAY TO COME TO ALBANY"

IT WAS WITH PRIDE IN HIS HEART—AND HIS heart in his mouth—that Al Smith set out for Albany on the first Tuesday of January in 1904. He arrived at nightfall to find the city blanketed in snow and the temperature fifteen below zero, but neither snow nor intense cold could cool the fever of excitement and anxiety within him. He felt as a fighter must feel climbing through the ropes for his first important bout. Behind him lay the weeks of preparation, the months, even years of anticipation. Now that was all over. On the morrow he would have to start proving himself —proving, one way or another, whether or not Tom Foley and the voters of the Second Assembly District had made a mistake in conferring their confidence upon him.

With him was Tom Caughlan, who represented the First Assembly District, covering territory adjacent to the Battery and ruled over by "Battery Dan" Finn. As they climbed down from the smoking car on the head end of the train, there was a slight commotion on the station platform behind them and they saw and recognized Governor Benjamin B. Odell, in top hat and fur-collared overcoat, being met by some friends. They watched, from the edge of the crowd of passengers grouped about the Governor, the deference with which he was received, the eagerness with which porters scrambled for his luggage; and, picking up their own handbags, they trailed the party out of the station, where a sleigh, drawn by a magnificently turned out pair of horses, awaited him.

Al turned to Caughlan.

"That's the way to come to Albany," he said.

Caughlan nodded and they walked up, through ice and snow, to Keeler's Hotel, where they had decided to put up until they could find cheaper quarters, since neither of them could afford to live at a hotel and maintain a home in New York on a salary of $1,500 a year.

That first night in Albany was filled with a terror for Al that had nothing to do with his approaching bow as a legislator. Curiously enough, for one who as a boy had spent so much time in close contact with the Fire Department and had dreamed, once upon a time, of being a fireman, it was a dread of fire that kept him wakeful and uneasy all that night.

He had read in the newspapers a day or two before of a fire in a Chicago hotel that had taken a number of lives, and this was recalled to his mind when, on walking into Keeler's, he saw a man piling logs on a roaring blaze in a huge fireplace in the lobby. He looked about him. What he saw was not reassuring, for the hotel did not appear to him to be a model of fireproofing.

To his dismay, he and Caughlan were assigned to a room on the seventh floor. Tom, who was tired, went to bed almost immediately, while Al occupied himself by apprehensively surveying his surroundings with a view to making a hasty exit in case of fire. The more he examined the layout, the more apprehensive he became.

"Tom," he said.

"Huh?"

Tom was half asleep.

"Wake up. I think we're in a fire trap."

Tom not only woke up but sat up.

"What put that in your head?" he asked.

"You read about that fire in Chicago the other day, didn't you? Well, if this place should catch fire while we are asleep, we'll be burned to death in our beds."

"Don't be silly."

"I'm not silly. I've been looking around. We're on the seventh floor and the nearest fire escape is at the end of the hall. If a fire should reach that hall before we woke up, we'd be cooked, I'm telling you."

"Well, what do you want me to do? The hotel is crowded and I know we can't get a room lower down or right next to a fire escape."

"How about a game of pinochle?" Al asked, hopefully.

"Pinochle! At this hour of night? Do you know we have to be up early in the morning and go out to the capitol?"

"I'd rather lose a little sleep than lose my life," Al said.

Grumbling, Tom got up and began to dress.

"Get the cards," he said.

"Thanks, Tom."

"Thanks, nothing. You'd keep me awake all night, anyway, so I might as well be enjoying myself."

So they sat up playing pinochle until five o'clock in the morning and then took turns sleeping until broad daylight, when they went down to breakfast. Then, sleepy-eyed, they walked to the Capitol.

Once within the doors of that historic building they were restored to complete wakefulness by the bustle going on about them as the legislature gathered to start a new term. The Democratic members of the Assembly constituted a tiny minority and met in the Assembly parlor, while to the startled eyes of the newcomers from New York the Assembly chamber itself seemed to bulge with Republicans.

About eleven o'clock, the oath was administered to the entire Assembly. This was the most thrilling moment Al ever had known, but it passed all too soon as the body moved into its first session. Suddenly he was plunged into a state of confusion from which he was not to emerge completely for a year or more. The complicated rules of procedure ... the astonishing number of bills that were introduced ... the language in which these bills were couched ... the wordy arguments that each pending act of legislation brought on ...

thoroughly bewildered him and at times frightened him. Conscientious, he took bills home with him at night—home to the furnished room that he and Tom Caughlan occupied in a house on Broadway—and pored over them in an attempt to find out what those who had written them really had in mind. Uneducated and unused to studying anything save his parts in the plays at St. James's, he could make neither head nor tail of most of them.

In the Assembly chamber, as an obscure member of a feeble minority he occupied a seat so far in the rear that visitors to the chamber had a better view of the proceedings than he did, and very often he couldn't hear what was going on. Not, he reflected, that that made much difference, since even when he could hear, he frequently didn't know what the speakers were talking about.

"Never make a promise you do not intend to keep," Foley had admonished him the day he left New York. And: "Don't open your mouth on the floor of the Assembly unless you have something to say."

He laughed bitterly to himself as he recalled that advice.

"Fat chance of me disregarding it," he muttered. "Nobody asks me to do any favors and nobody gives me a chance to say anything, no matter what."

Was this the Assembly of which he had daydreamed so long? This the glory that he thought had been promised to him on the day when the voters had swept him into office? He was ready to believe Judge Allison was right in his low appraisal of assemblymen, especially those who were not lawyers. Further disillusionment assailed him on the night of the Governor's reception to the legislature in the Executive Mansion soon after the opening of the session.

This was his first opportunity to wear his evening clothes, and he looked forward eagerly to an enjoyable evening in the warmth and charm of the mansion. It would be something to tell Katie and his mother about, something to brag about to the boys at the Downtown Tammany Club, something to look back on and remember for a very long time.

Arrayed in what he always called his spike tails and top hat, he arrived at the mansion with four other legislators. They were guided through a rear entrance, presented to the Governor and his wife and members of his staff—and ushered out the front door. Their evening of charm had lasted three minutes and they were on their way to the Hotel Ten Eyck, where they had a little party of their own.

Puzzled by the speed with which the Governor had brushed off his guests—Smith and his companions had been rushed through no more rapidly than perhaps five thousand others— Al asked one of the older men what it was all about.

"I thought the Governor was on the level when he invited us," he said. "I thought there would be just members of the Senate and Assembly there. Who were all those other people?"

The older man smiled.

"You'll learn about these things after a while," he said. "The Governor's reception to the legislature is just a gesture on his part. He doesn't mean anything by it and we know it, but it's an old custom that he can't drop—and, of course, we can't drop it, either. A few of those other people were friends and acquaintances of the Governor. Most of the rest were sightseers and gate crushers."

Al shook his head.

"If I ever become governor," he said, "I'll change the rules. I'll have a reception that really will be for the legislators and their families, with no outsiders butting in. I'll—"

"Very interesting," one of his companions said. "And just when do you expect to become governor, Mr. Smith?"

They all laughed.

"One of these days," Al said.

All in fun? Not quite. Not on Al's part. Somewhere in the back of his mind, perhaps unrealized until that moment, the thought had been forming. Oh, on his first day in Albany he had sent his mother a postcard bearing a picture of the Executive Mansion and on it he had written:

"This is a picture of the Governor's residence. I'm going to work hard and stick to the ideals you taught me and some day—maybe—I'll occupy this house."

But any young man might have written that. This thought was different, serious. Now he had put it into words. Mind, he did not say:

"If I were governor..."

Or:

"If I were in his place..."

He said:

"If I ever become governor..."

Where had it come from? Sitting in the Assembly chamber, listening to one of the other members droning...or ranting ...over some bill? Climbing the long steps to the Capitol doors on some frosty morning? Looking at the lights twinkling in the mansion as darkness settled over Albany and he hurried to his furnished room on Broadway, clutching his homework, as he was beginning to call the bills he took with him to study?

Certainly the thought of one day becoming governor had not been in his mind when he arrived from New York. Then his mind had been filled with thoughts of his own fancied importance as a representative of the voters of his district... and a sense of trepidation over the grave problems with which he expected to grapple so soon. But it was there now and it never was to leave him completely, and it would grow into a driving ambition that one day would be fulfilled.

8: THE PSYCHOLOGY OF TOM FOLEY

HELPFUL IN THE FULFILLMENT OF THAT AMbition would be the experience he was gaining now as a virtually unnoticed and absolutely inarticulate freshman assemblyman, puzzling over what he heard and read and chafing under the inactivity that had been forced upon him. But now he was conscious only of the bleakness of his life as a legislator, which was lightened only by week ends with his family.

When he was in New York—he went to the city every Thursday or Friday and returned to Albany on Monday morning—he divided his time between his home and the club. There he talked with Foley, who smiled at his impatience with the role he was playing and encouraged him with predictions of the bright future he was building for himself; and with constituents who called upon him to ask for favors. Happily, most of the favors had a strictly local angle and he was able to grant them, for although he was a nobody in Albany, he was not without influence at home. His willingness to help those who came to him and the tangible results of his efforts—to get jobs, or salary increases, to ward off rivals of other political faiths or to stall creditors —these strengthened his position and assured him of even greater support at the polls than he had received in his first trial by ballot. Refreshed by a visit to New York, he would go back to Albany with a firm intention of breaking down the obstacles that awaited him there—and by the end of the week he would be discouraged again.

At last the term dragged to a close . . . and he had the sour knowledge that there was nothing in the record, aside from his regular attendance at the sessions and his regular party vote on every project considered by the Assembly, to show that he ever had been in Albany. He had served on no committees, however unimportant. He had made no speeches. He had, in fact, done nothing. Even the votes he had cast had had no effect on any legislation that had been enacted. For all that his presence had meant, he might just as well have spent his days and nights at the Downtown Tammany Club, which, in all truth, he fervently wished he had.

There was, however, no question that he would be re-elected. He had pleased Foley by the regularity of his vote, his unbroken silence on the floor, and his strict attention to his duties on his week ends in New York. He had gained steadily in the favor of the voters, and although he did not realize it ... and Foley thought it wise not to say anything to him about it ... he was being watched closely by Charlie Murphy. And so, in November, he won again on election day—won so easily that his opponents, who had no real hope of beating him, anyway, knew the jig was up as soon as the early returns were in.

Through the early months of the 1905 term, Al felt that he still was getting nowhere and that he never would break through the fog of legislative ignorance that closed about him whenever he entered Albany. Somewhat to his surprise, he was appointed to serve on two committees, but even that made him grin sardonically. The committees were on banks and on public lands and forestry. Banks? What did he know of banks or banking law? As for forests, he'd never so much as seen a forest. Well, at least he could listen to the other members of the committees and learn something. As a matter of fact, he learned much—more than he appreciated at the time. This, in common with all the other seemingly baffling experiences he was having, would yield a solid payoff in days to come.

As spring wore on, his dissatisfaction with his position at Albany grew to a point where he felt that he could not continue in the Assembly beyond that term. Sometimes sadly, sometimes bitterly, he complained to Foley that he was wasting time. That no matter how hard he tried to comprehend the way the game was played at the capital, he could understand little and accomplish nothing. Foley, taking him along easily, gentling him as a wise trainer gentles a highstrung, promising two-year-old race horse, usually managed to revive his spirits and give him a hopeful slant on the future. One Friday night in June at the club the boss saw that he would have to tighten his grip on the young man, pull him up sharply—and then send him whirling on his way. That, or find some other spot for him, or see him peter out completely as a political prospect.

Tom wasn't so much afraid of the last possibility, however. Al had too much character to quit, as some other young men he had groomed had done when things broke badly for them or, as in this case, failed to break at all, one way or the other. But he felt that he must have a plain talk with him to get him properly straightened out.

It was too late at night to start working on Al then. Better get him in the early morning, before he had too much time to think of the troubles he had.

"Meet me at Holtz's for breakfast tomorrow morning," he said.

The next morning they sat at a corner table at Holtz's, a restaurant on lower Broadway much favored by politicians.

"Now let's have it," Tom said. "Everything that's on your mind."

Trying to find words in which to wrap his woes, Al discovered he had little to say. He didn't like being an assemblyman. He was halfway through his second term and the only ones who seemed to know he ever had been to Albany were fellows like Tom Caughlan who were friends of his.

"And the landlady of the house where Tom and I room,"

he added, with a wry smile. "She looks me up every week to get the room rent."

Even the Democratic leader of the Assembly and the other members of the committees to which he had been appointed seemed to have no interest in him beyond his vote on a measure or his nod of assent at the end of a discussion.

Foley listened intently until he had finished. Then:

"Is that all?"

"Yes."

"Well," the boss said, "if that's the way you feel about it, maybe I can do something in the way of getting a job for you down here. Mayor McClellan has asked me to suggest a man for the post of superintendent of buildings. How would that suit you?"

Al's eyes lighted.

"That sounds all right," he said.

Foley looked at him narrowly.

"And then what?" he asked. "What—after that?"

Al was surprised by the question.

"Why, I don't know," he said. "I don't know just what you mean. If I do a good job there, there should be another place for me later on."

"You want to get ahead, don't you? You want to be a big man in this town some day, eh? Well, I gave you a start in that direction. I know it isn't easy for you now. It never is easy for a beginner at Albany, for there is a lot to learn there and you can't learn it in a couple of weeks—or even a couple of years. I still think that you're on the right track. Your popularity is growing in the district all the time, and whether you think so or not, you're not wasting your time. You haven't had any complaints from me, have you?" he asked with a smile.

"No," Al said, smiling, too.

"But if you think you'd rather chuck it and take this building job, maybe you're right. Maybe you're right in thinking that Albany is too tough for you."

Neither had eaten much. They were letting their ham and eggs grow cold.

"Let's forget it for a while," Tom said, picking up his knife and fork. "Let's eat. And I don't want you to make any decision today. Think it over. There's no hurry about it. The building job can wait."

Al had not made up his mind what to do when he went back to Albany early Monday morning. But within a week or so, he knew what he would do. He would accept the thinly veiled challenge Foley had hurled at him.

"Maybe ... Albany is too tough for you," the boss had said.

Well, he'd show Tom—and all the world—that it wasn't. He'd attack his problems even harder than he had before. He'd find out how things were done at Albany—and he'd do them.

He was smiling and cheerful when next he met Foley at the club.

"I'm all right now, Tom," he said. "You've heard the last squawk from me. I don't want the building job. I want to go back to Albany next year ... if I can."

"As long as you want to, you can," Foley said. "You're the only one who could prevent that."

There was another overwhelming vote for Al in November, and in January of 1906 he was sworn in for his third term. Now the fog in which he had been enveloped for two terms was thinning and he was beginning to see things clearly. Of tremendous importance to him was the fact that James W. Wadsworth, who had been elected speaker that year, had become attracted to him. With full confidence in him—more than the older Democratic members had evinced, indeed—Wadsworth, although a Republican, engineered his appointment to some of the major committees. Smith and Wadsworth always would be at odds politically and in time to come would take each other to task sharply on issues before the Assembly, but it was an enduring friendship that began between them early in 1906, a friendship that in no wise could be affected by matters political.

Spurred by the interest that Wadsworth and other influential members of the lower house were showing in him, and encouraged by the new and firmer grasp he was getting on the measures that came before that body, Al worked tirelessly. No longer was he bored by speeches he couldn't understand but he sought hard to get the meaning of them. He haunted the libraries, pored over lawbooks that, by their very formidable appearance, would have frightened him off even a year before, and studied night and day that he might improve himself and thus serve his constituents more intelligently.

It wasn't all work and no play, however. Feeling surer of himself as the term advanced, he found time to relax and enjoy himself on one or two nights a week. His fellow assemblymen had discovered that he had a great fund of amusing stories which he told well, that he knew the words of all the popular songs, old and new, which he sang in a slightly nasal but not unpleasing voice, and that he could dance more than passably well. He had moved from the rooming house to the Ten Eyck Hotel, and he was the life of many a party at the hotel. Mostly he found his greatest enjoyment sitting around with a few of his friends, smoking a cigar, drinking beer, raising his voice in song.

The next two years were to be eventful ones in his life and to mark very definitely the progress he was making. In 1907 his voice was heard on the floor of the Assembly for the first time as he took part in discussions of amendments to the charter of the city of New York, and so clearly and forcefully did he speak that he was appointed as a member of the committee to revise that charter. In 1908 he met Charlie Murphy for the first time. He was inclined to believe, always, that it was a mere casual meeting, which meant nothing to him, since it was not until three years later that he got to know the Big Boss well. The circumstances were such as to make it appear that way to him, as they were introduced while swimming at Quogue, near Murphy's famous summer home at Good Ground. Al was spending the summer at Good Ground, too, and friends brought them together. Al thought the meeting had made no impress on Murphy's mind. Actually, Murphy was very much—although at that time secretly—interested in the young man of whom Tom Foley had spoken to him approvingly, and at that meeting, brief as it was, Murphy sized him up thoroughly.

"He is a nice young fellow," someone said to Murphy. "He has a lot of ability. It is too bad he isn't a college man."

Murphy smiled.

"If he was a college man," he said, "he wouldn't be Al Smith."

9: A TRAGEDY—AND A TURNING POINT

THE YEARS WERE PASSING SWIFTLY NOW ... 1908 ... 1909 ... 1910. In January of 1911 when Al Smith went to Albany to begin his eighth term as an assemblyman, the Democratic party was riding high. In the preceding November its entire ticket, headed by its gubernatorial nominee, John Alden Dix, an upstate lumberman, had been elected. For the first time in nineteen years both houses were in control of the Democrats, and at the behest of Charlie Murphy, Al was selected as leader of the Assembly and appointed chairman of the Committee on Ways and Means, the most powerful group within the lower house.

He was in his thirty-eighth year and was living now in the home with which he was, in time, to be so closely identified that there is a rather widespread belief he was born there: at 25 Oliver Street. The Smiths had lived for a time at 28 Oliver, but the growing family—Catherine Alice was born in 1904 and Arthur William in 1907—had made roomier quarters necessary, and with the help of the young men from the Downtown Tammany Club and the small boys of the neighborhood, they had moved directly across the street to a house owned by St. James's Church. There the fifth and last child, Walter Joseph, was born on December 28, 1909.

He who once had been on the point of quitting the Assembly in despair because he found it so difficult to understand what was going on during its deliberations ... the nobody whom Tom Foley wisely had gagged through his first two terms and to whom no one had cared to listen, anyway ... had become one of the most intelligent of legislators and one of the clearest, soundest, and most forceful speakers in either house. Murphy had picked him shrewdly as the man best fitted to keep the other Democrats in line on sharply controversial measures, and although he never had served as a member of the Ways and Means Committee, Murphy knew that he would direct it ably. Opposition newspapers hammered at him, of course, calling him a mere tool of the Boss, but in spite of their attacks his popularity was growing constantly, not only within his own party but with an element of the Republicans.

With him in Albany now, starting a second term as an assemblyman and living with him at the Ten Eyck, was a young man of whom he was very fond and for whom he foresaw a bright future. The young man was James J. Walker, who one day was to become world famous as the glamorous Jimmy Walker, Mayor of the City of New York, but now, under Al's tutelage, just learning his way about the Assembly. Al had known Jimmy's father for years and had known Jimmy since he was a little boy.

"The first time I ever saw him," Al recalled, "was on a New Year's Day visit at the Walker home in St. Luke's Place. I didn't see much of him on that occasion, for he was a very little fellow and was put to bed early." Then, in recognition of the grown-up Jimmy's propensity for night life, he added: "That probably was the last time he was put to bed early."

When Jimmy was elected to the Assembly in November of 1909, Al had promised his father that he would look after him carefully at Albany and now he was fulfilling that promise.

"He did it thoroughly, as he did everything," Jimmy was to say, long years afterward. "My father went with me to the Grand Central the day I was leaving, and Al was there to meet us. He practically took me aboard the train by the hand, and our rooms were in readiness for us when we reached Albany. He introduced me to all the people he thought I should know—and kept me away from those he thought I shouldn't. It was a wonderful break for me and I never forgot his kindness."

A wonderful break—and a sharp contrast to Al's own entrance into Albany seven years before when, friendless save for Tom Caughlan, as little known and unimportant as himself, he spent that first terror-filled night at Keeler's Hotel and then went to live in a cheap rooming house. And Al was as happy as Jimmy in their association. He had the companionship of one who, like himself, was fond of the theater and of laughter and song—hadn't Jimmy stopped off long enough in Tin Pan Alley to write "Will You Love Me in December As You Do in May?" He had, too, Jimmy's lively assistance in the Assembly chamber. No such restraint as Foley had put on Smith in the beginning had been put on Walker. Jimmy's wit and eloquence were heard many times in the 1910 session, and Jimmy was an apt legislative pupil and a dead game, stand-up fighter in a pinch. Indeed, before the session was over, he was of tremendous help to Smith in delivering telling blows against the reeling Republican majority, and some of the Republican newspapers were denouncing them as scoundrels and urging their defeat at the next election.

Scant attention had been given to these urgings, however, and now Al and Jimmy were in Albany again, more powerful than before, and working harder than ever to effect the passing of measures to which, by party platform, they were committed.

Smith's progress, steady as it had been, was about to be accelerated. His reputation had outgrown the Downtown Tammany Club and the Second Assembly District. He was well known throughout New York City, and Murphy regarded him as the brightest of his "four bright young men," as they were known in Albany: Smith, Bob Wagner, Jim Foley, and Aaron Levy. Yet so far as the upper regions of the state were concerned, he was but a name, and his name was not too well known, at that, save by those who were politically minded. Now he was to be projected into a position where all would know him and from which he would sponsor—and put through—legislation affecting the lives of the countless thousands of men, women, and children employed in the factories, canneries, and other industrial plants of the state.

There would be a time when he would look back and say, at least to himself, that he had profited politically from the aftermath of that which occurred on March 26, 1911, to such an extent that it could be said his whole political life turned on it. He did not like to say it, even to himself, because the event itself was a great tragedy that took more than one hundred lives. But there it was, and he couldn't do anything about it but he could—and did—see to it that nothing like it ever would happen again, not only in New York state but in every other state, because the legislation he laid out for New York was a pattern for the entire nation.

Late in the afternoon of Saturday, March 26, 1911, some six hundred employees of the Triangle Shirtwaist Company were at work on the eighth, ninth, and tenth floors of the Asch Building, on the corner of Washington Place and Greene Street in New York City. Nearly five hundred of them were girls from homes on the East Side, within walking distance of the shop. The day's work was nearly done and they were talking among themselves of their plans for their day of rest on the morrow . . . and someone in the tenth floor workroom lighted a cigarette and thoughtlessly tossed the still burning match into the ankle deep litter near one of the sewing machines.

There was a puff of smoke, a sheet of flame . . . and panic. Girls and men rushed for the fire escape and found the door was locked. Another door, leading to a hallway, opened inward, and a struggling mass of frightened workers prevented it from being opened at all. The cries of those on the uppermost floor, the smell of smoke, the heat of the flames fed by flimsy cloth . . . these served to spread the panic to the floors beneath. Some escaped from the eighth and ninth floors. Others on those floors, rushing about wildly, were crushed to death or overcome by the heavy smoke that swirled through hallways and elevator shafts. Girls trapped by flame and smoke leaped from the windows as firemen, unable to reach them even with extension ladders, hastened to spread life nets. Bodies smashed against the sidewalks and tore through sidewalk gratings. Scores of those penned above were burned to death or suffocated. When the dead were counted, there were 141—125 of them girls.

Horror swept the city as panic had swept the victims of the fire. Investigations were launched immediately with two purposes in view—one to fix responsibility for the disaster, the other to make certain there would never be a repetition of it. Henry Moskowitz, representing the Committee of Safety, and John Kingsbury of the Association for Improvement of the Condition of the Poor, went to Albany and appealed to Smith to help them by bringing about the enactment of legislation to protect workers, not only in New York City but elsewhere in the state, against a recurrence of such a tragedy.

Smith conferred with them and with Bob Wagner, leader of the Senate, and as a result bills were introduced by Smith in the Assembly and by Wagner in the Senate calling for a joint commission to look into the matter and, after a careful study, to recommend laws to guard the health and safety of factory workers. There already were, of course, such laws on the books, but for one reason or another they were not enforceable. Smith and Wagner wanted some that would stick ... and were determined to get them.

The bills were passed and the commission was appointed. On it were two senators, three assemblymen and four citizens named by the governor. As one of the assemblymen and vicechairman of the commission, Smith gave every hour he could spare from his tasks in Albany to a thorough investigation, covering the state from one end to the other. He didn't think of it then, being concerned only with stern duties imposed upon him, but for the first time he was seeing the far reaches of the state, and those who inhabited them—employers, employees, town, county, and state officials, newspaper editors— were seeing him. Seeing him and sizing him up and remembering him.

Unmindful of the attention he attracted and the impression he made on those with whom he came in contact, he poked into the nooks and crannies of the state's industrial system, and much that he saw displeased or revolted him and he swore that he would work unceasingly to correct the faults uncovered by the commission. The powers conferred upon the commission were broad, and he seized upon them and made the most of them. Opposition from some of the factory owners, who were politically intrenched at Albany, first shocked him and then spurred him to greater efforts. Much of this opposition came from the owners of canneries where, it was discovered, women and even children worked as much as sixteen hours a day, seven days a week.

The battle with the canneries was centered on a bill that required all employers to give their workers at least one day's rest a week. Incredibly, the tin can tycoons wanted their establishments exempted. Smith dealt with that outrageous plea and assured the passage of the bill in the Assembly with the briefest speech ever made from the floor of the Assembly chamber.

"I have read carefully the commandment, 'Remember the Sabbath Day, to keep it holy,'" he said, "but I am unable to find any language in it that says 'except in the canneries.'"

His labors as a member of the commission, his courageous fight against the most powerful interests that attempted to block it, and the tremendous good that came of it, due largely to his unflagging zeal, marked him out as one who sincerely had at heart the welfare of the overworked and underprivileged. By a strict devotion to a task that had clutched at his heart, he had earned countless new friends, and those who had called him a mere tool of Boss Murphy were humbled.

10: MAKING FRIENDS—AND LOSING SOME

THAT WAS A BUSY YEAR, 1911. ATTENDANCE AT the regular sessions of the legislature ... trips with the wide-ranging Factory Commission ... weekly conferences with Murphy and other leaders at Delmonico's in New York ... the straightening out of tangles in the not always smoothly working Democratic majority at Albany ... these crowded him for time, day and night. And yet, because it was important to him, he never, when in New York, missed a night at the Downtown Tammany Club, where he listened patiently to all who went to him with pleas for help and helped those whom he could.

There were, as there always had been and always would be, those who needed coal ... or ice ... or rent ... or bail money. Who wanted a cop pulled off a complaint or a magistrate softened up or a creditor placated—with or without money. There was a fireman who wanted a transfer or a policeman who wanted to be a sergeant ... or a sergeant who wanted to be a lieutenant. Or somebody had died and the undertaker wanted more than promises from his relatives before putting the deceased to rest, and would the Assemblyman ...

Most of all, perhaps, the job seekers gave him trouble. No longer did his constituents ask only for a chance to wield a pick and shovel or drive a truck or turn on the street lamps at night or find out what it was that clogged a sewer. The Fourth Ward was growing up intellectually, and the boys ... and girls ... were aiming higher. They wanted civil service jobs or jobs with the insurance or the public service companies. He did the best he could for them, and sometimes they failed him and generally when that happened the resulting bitterness was on their side, not his.

He lost a friend and made an enemy, for instance, because he was too considerate to tell the truth to a man for whose daughter he had obtained a position with one of the insurance companies. The father came to him one night and complained that his daughter had been dismissed for no reason whatever and he virtually demanded that Al have her reinstated. Al promised to see what he could do for the girl and, true to his promise, called up the manager of her department the next day.

"You know I would do anything in the world for you, Mr. Smith," the manager said. "But please don't ask me to take that girl back."

"Why not?" Al asked.

"Because she is absolutely incompetent. In fact, while I don't like to say this about anybody you sent to me, she is a dope. She can't do even the simplest things around the office. I have given her every chance, but she's hopeless. Ask the girls she worked with and they will tell you the same thing."

That night the father called on Al again. Al had two choices: to repeat to him what the manager had said or simply to tell him he could do nothing for the girl and let him draw his own conclusions. To give him the truth would be to belittle the hapless girl in the eyes of her father, which was the last thing in the world he wanted to do.

"Well?" the father demanded.

Al shrugged.

"I guess it's no use," he said. "I can't get her back."

The father laughed scornfully.

"A fine guy!" he said. "A fine guy!"

He walked from the room and never spoke to Al again. Moreover, it was suspected in the district that forever after he voted the Republican ticket.

He wasn't the only one who built up a grievance against Smith in his mind and clung to it tenaciously.

"There are guys in this neighborhood right now," Robbie Weisberger, the shoe merchant, said, not so long ago, "who still are sore at Al. You know why they are sore at him, don't you? Because he didn't wrap the world up for them and give it to them on a silver platter."

But for the most part he was able to satisfy the demands upon him and not only to hold but to build upon the support of the voters. A majority of them knew there wasn't anything in his power he wouldn't do for them, and they were as loyal to him as he was to them. Still remembered gratefully by a group of them is a night in Brassell's saloon, long since vanished but then flourishing on the corner of Catherine and Madison. Racing, under a heavy fire by Governor Charles Evans Hughes, had folded up in New York state in 1910, and now, early in 1911, it was plain that the tracks would not reopen that year. Among Brassell's clientele were numerous bookmakers' clerks, cashiers, runners, track employees, touts, and assorted horse players who, having followed the horses to the winter tracks, had come back to New York in a desperate hope that somehow there would be racing that spring at Jamaica, Aqueduct, and Belmont Park. Now they knew the awful truth. They were standing along the bar at Brassell's or grouped about the tables, discussing their dreadful plight, when Al walked in. He had known most of them all his life or, in the case of the younger ones, all their lives.

Racing meant nothing to him; nor any other form of gambling, save penny-ante poker with his friends. Nor could he understand how anyone willingly would depend upon so precarious a business as racing for a living or, even worse, try to make his living by betting on the horses. Still, these were his friends and he sympathized with them in their troubles and was eager to help them if he could with advice and, if they took it, with direct action.

"Why don't you go to work?" he asked, bluntly.

Some of them were shocked at the very thought. Others looked at him aggrieved.

"We work," they said, stoutly.

"Sure. You work. But at what? The truth of the matter is that, all of a sudden, you have no jobs—unless you want to go tramping around the country. Why don't you get jobs around here? If any of you is willing to try it, I'll help you."

Most of them declined the offer, preferring to scramble along as best they could ... to make book on the horses running elsewhere ... to follow the horses ... to stick it out, somehow, until the horses returned to New York. Seven saw the wisdom of his suggestion and seized upon his offer to help them. He lined up jobs for all seven, aiding five of them to get into civil service.

Al's own political position was secure, but there were others in the district who had to fight hard to hold their jobs. He gave his support to those he believed were deserving of it and threw his weight against those who were not. Foley, still at the height of his powers as leader, valued Al's advice more than that of any of his other lieutenants and not only called him into conference on squabbles within the district but took him with him on frequent visits to Tammany Hall or private meetings with other leaders throughout the city.

Lively times in the old neighborhood ... and lively times at Albany, too. Times to be serious ... and times to laugh. Times to riddle an opponent on the floor of the Assembly with ridicule, and times, by the interjection of a wisecrack, to take the heat off a debate and, having made the other members laugh, to get them back to the pressing business at hand.

Two of the most oft-repeated tales of Smith's years in the Assembly came out of the 1911 terms. The goat of one was an assemblyman named Pratt, who was from Washington County and constantly heckled Smith during his speeches, always referring to him as the "Tammany Leader."

One night Al was in the midst of a serious attack on a proposed amendment to the Workman's Compensation Act, and Pratt rose in his place and asked:

"Mr. Tammany Leader, what good is the Workman's Compensation Act to the three hundred and fifty thousand men who are out of work in this state?"

The hour was late and Al was weary. Turning to the Speaker, he said:

"Mr. Speaker, I was walking down Park Row not long ago and a man said to me:

" 'Al, which would you rather be, a hammock full of white door knobs, a cellar full of stepladders, or a piece of dry ice?'

"And I said:

" 'I would rather be a fish, because no matter how thick plate glass is, you can always break it with a hammer.' "

Pratt was dazed.

"I don't get the point," he said.

Smith turned to him angrily.

"There was just as much sense in my answer as there was in your question," he snapped.

On another occasion, there was a bitter fight being waged on the floor over the proposed removal of the Commissioner of Jurors of Niagara county and Al was standing off the verbal assaults of three Republican assemblymen, Jesse Phillips, Edward Merritt, and Fred Hammond. The row was at its peak when Assemblyman Wende of Buffalo asked if he might interrupt. Naturally thinking he had something to add to the debate, the combatants said that he might.

"I have just heard," he said, "that Cornell won the boat race."

"That doesn't mean a thing to me," Merritt said. "I'm a Yale man."

"To me, either," Hammond said. "I'm a Harvard man."

"That goes for me," Phillips said. "I'm a U. of M. man."

Everybody looked at Al.

"It's all right with me," he said. "I'm an F.F.M. man."

"What's that, Al?" somebody shouted.

"Fulton Fish Market," Al said. "Now let's get on with the argument."

It was also during the 1911 term that Al thoughtlessly broke the rule that Foley had laid down for him: "Never make a promise unless you can keep it."

An assemblyman whose East Side district was a haven for pushcart peddlers introduced a bill that was calculated to lighten the lives of many of his constituents by making it legal for them to ply their trade anywhere, and asked Al to support it.

"You know what they're up against, Al," he said. "The cops shove them around or take petty graft from them, and it's time they got a break."

Al's inherent sympathy for the underdog got the better of him, and for once he failed to study a bill before committing himself to it—or against it.

"Sure," he said. "I'll go for it."

"And you'll see the rest of the boys, eh?"

"Sure. I'll line them up."

He was sincere, as always. But when he started to line the boys up, one of them said to him:

"Do you realize what this bill means?"

"Yes," Al said. "It means that a lot of poor devils who work themselves half to death every day will get a break."

"That's right. It also means that a peddler can push his cart up to the very door of a store selling the same wares he's carrying—and undersell the poor storekeeper who has to pay rent and light and heat bills. Or he can make his pitch in front of your house—or mine or anybody else's in any town from New York to Buffalo and back—and if a cop tries to chase him, he can tell the cop to go jump in the lake. I'm for anybody that's trying to make a living—including the storekeepers. But I don't want anybody thrown into unfair competition—and I don't want a guy to haul a pushcart up in front of my house and stay there all day if he feels like it."

Al nodded.

"You're right," he said.

In all conscience, he couldn't ask the other members of his party in the Assembly to vote for the bill—and in all conscience, he couldn't refuse to vote for it himself. And so, when the bill came to a vote, the confident sponsor of it was shocked. All the Democrats voted against it but Smith. Bewildered at first, then indignant, he asked the Speaker's permission to say something. The request having been granted, he yelled:

"I just want to say that Assemblyman Smith was in favor of my bill. In the pig's eye!"

11: SPEAKER OF THE ASSEMBLY

THE DEMOCRATS RECEIVED A SETBACK IN THE voting for assemblymen in the fall of 1911, so that the lower house once more was controlled by the Republicans in 1912 and Al, who had been majority leader the year before, now led the minority. This diminution of his power created some difficulties in bringing about the passage of new factory laws that he introduced, but with the aid of Edward Merritt, the majority leader, he was able to get most of them through. Merritt, who frequently fought Al on the floor, was as frequently on his side, especially where social legislation was concerned. They were very good friends, and Merritt, who represented a district in upstate St. Lawrence County, often made week-end trips to New York with Al and walked the streets of the East Side with him, thus gaining a better appreciation of the problems and needs of the city dwellers than most of the legislators from the rural districts.

In November of 1912 a Democratic landslide swept the state. The normal Republican vote was split by the entrance of the Progressive party into the field, and William Sulzer of New York City, who had been drafted from Congress to run for governor on the Democratic ticket, was elected, along with a preponderant majority in both the Senate and the Assembly. And now Smith reaped the highest political honor that he had yet known: he was chosen as speaker of the Assembly.

The day he was inducted in that post his wife, his mother, and his five children were present. He felt, justly, that he had come a long way from the docks and the fish market;

and if, as he was to say later, he believed he had reached the peak of his political career, it is understandable, for the speaker of the Assembly is endowed with almost unlimited power in that body's shaping of laws and spending of the state's money. But that feeling that he had gone as far as he could would pass away and he would look ahead once more, and the lurking thought that one day he might be governor would spur him again.

The term over which he presided as speaker was a long and stormy one. The last of the factory bills for which Al had battled unceasingly were passed. So was an amendment to the state constitution granting suffrage to women. Al was opposed to that originally, not only because at the time he personally thought there was no need for it but because he believed he reflected the views of both men and women in his district. When he became convinced that a majority of the voters in the state favored it, he cast his vote for it.

The high spot of the term, however, was the impeachment and removal of the new governor. Smith had opposed the choice of Sulzer and made no bones about his lack of enthusiasm for the man, even after the election, and yet, possibly because he foresaw that the impeachment of the Governor by his own party would make excellent capital for the Republicans, and possibly because he believed Sulzer was being persecuted, it was with reluctance that he voted for it. Charged with a violation of the Corrupt Practices Act in connection with his campaign fund, and tried before the Senate and the judges of the Court of Appeals, Sulzer was found guilty and automatically removed, being succeeded by the lieutenant governor, Martin H. Glynn.

Sulzer, aware that Smith had been against him from the beginning, and alleging that Al had wholeheartedly entered into what he called a frame-up rigged by Murphy because he would not bow to the Boss's will, refused to quit fighting simply because he had been counted out. That fall he ran for the Assembly from the Sixth District in New York and was elected. During the campaign he invaded the Second District in an attempt to undermine and defeat Smith—and barely escaped with his life.

In November of 1914 the Republicans were catapulted back into power, recapturing both houses of the legislature and putting in the governor's chair Charles S. Whitman, who, as district attorney of New York County, had won national recognition by sending Police Lieutenant Charles Becker and four gunmen—Dago Frank, Whitey Lewis, Gyp the Blood, and Lefty Louie—to the electric chair for the murder of Herman Rosenthal, a gambler. Once more Al controlled only the minority in the Assembly in 1915, but by his excellent work there and the role he played in the Constitutional Convention that year, he added greatly to his stature.

No higher praise could have been given to him than that which came from Elihu Root, the convention's chairman, and from George W. Wickersham—and no more sincere, because, both being Republicans, they could not be suspected of political bias.

"Of all the men in the convention," Root said, "Alfred E. Smith was the best informed on the business of New York state."

And Wickersham added:

"He was the most useful man in the convention."

12: WITHDRAWAL FROM ALBANY

AL HAD SERVED CONTINUOUSLY IN THE AS-
sembly for twelve years. From an unknown, he had
become a person of prominence and importance, not only in
his own community but throughout the state, yet for all the
work he had done and all the honors he had earned, he was
still a relatively poor man. Often hard pressed to meet his
bills, for his family was growing and living expenses were
mounting rapidly, he accepted gratefully his party's nomination as sheriff of New York County in the fall of 1915. This
office carried, at the time, a salary of $12,000 and half the
fees collected.

His nomination was roundly applauded. Even the Citizens'
Union, which in times past had assailed him, and the newspapers that once had characterized him as boss-ridden, joined
in the acclaim, having given belated recognition to the
services he had rendered at Albany. Now, for the first time,
his appeal for votes extended beyond the Second Assembly
District and he launched a county-wide campaign. This had
its beginning in an Old Home Night in Oliver Street,
where his first speech was punctuated with reports of fireworks, and preceded and followed by the music of brass
bands. The street was gaily illuminated with lanterns from
Chinatown, and in the Downtown Tammany Club, Tom
Foley smiled benignly on the wholehearted sendoff by the
old neighborhood to the man whose career he had sponsored.

The earnest, often vivid campaign whirled to a close the
night before election and resulted in an overwhelming vote
in Al's favor. This led to another rousing demonstration in

Buffalo Bill and Annie Oakley (signatures)

Al Smith as Annie Oakley and Judge James Hoyer as Buffalo Bill
at a Costume Party during the Democratic Convention in 1908

The St. James' Players in a Revival of *The Shaughraun* in 1916. Jimmie Walker is fifth from the left
in the second row and Al Smith is second from the right in the same row

Oliver Street, and Al, flushed with victory and assured of a greatly augmented income for the next two years, promptly let contracts for an addition to his home, although it remained the property of the church.

Once installed in office on January 1, 1916, he was not altogether happy. The job had its compensations, of course. He no longer had to commute between Oliver Street and Albany but could be home every night, with his cherished wife and children about him. And he could watch, sometimes unbelieving, the rapid expansion of his bank account, which meant new comforts, new luxuries—such as his first automobile—and that measure of security he never had known before and the lack of which so often had worried him. Yet he freely confessed he missed the action at Albany, and on long drowsy afternoons in the sheriff's office he frequently found himself wondering what the boys in the Assembly were doing. He wished that he could be embroiled once more in one of those arguments, so dear to his heart, with—well, his friend Ed Merritt, for instance.

There was, for him, a nostalgic touch in an event that year that had nothing to do with his political career. One night when he was home, his friend Father Curry, the pastor of St. James's, called on him.

"Al," Father Curry said, "every time I've needed money for the parish I've called on you and a few like you. But I can't keep going back to you all the time. I have an idea and I'd like to hear what you think of it."

"What is it?"

"I thought if we could revive the old St. James Players, getting together as many of the old boys and girls as we could, and put on one of the shows for which you were famous, we might be able to make enough money out of two or three performances to carry us for a long while. What do you think?"

"It might be the ham in me," Al said, "but I think it's a great idea."

"Fine! Then I'll leave it to you," Father Curry said.

Al, who was used to having things left to him, scarcely nodded. He already was thinking of the old days, the old boys and girls. Knowing where this or that one was, wondering where he could find some of the others, counting off mournfully those who had died.

News that the St. James Players were to be gathered once more spread quickly through the old neighborhood. Henry McCaddin ... Tom Nolan ... Michael Daly ... all the old-timers were delighted as they met at Smith's house to discuss plans for the revival.

"What will we play, Al?" McCaddin asked.

"Why, *The Shaughraun,* of course," Al said.

"You'll be Corry Kinchela, naturally," Tom Nolan said.

"Naturally. And you'll thrill the audience as you used to as Harvey Duff."

"But who," McCaddin wanted to know, "is going to play Robert Folliott?"

That stumped them. Robert Folliott was the hero, a young and handsome man. They looked from one to the other—and got nowhere, for none of them was young and none was handsome. They ran over a list of possibilities and could hit on none that had the necessary qualifications. Suddenly Al said:

"I've got it! He's a ringer but nobody will mind, because he is young and handsome and I know he'll be swell in the part."

"Who's that?"

"Jimmy Walker."

"Wonderful—if he'll do it."

"Of course he'll do it," Al said.

Of course he would, too. And so the company was assembled, parts were distributed, and rehearsals were begun. Contrarily enough, business became brisk in the sheriff's office just about that time and Al had to miss out on most of the rehearsals, but it was remarkable how well he remem-

bered the lines he hadn't read for years. Besides, he had the
children to help him. Most eager in this respect was Arthur,
who was nine years old. He was going over the lines with Al
one night and at one point stopped and wrinkled his brow.

"Well, go ahead," Al said. "What's the next line?"

The next line was: "Hush. Be quiet. 'Tis Conn."

Arthur, his newly begun struggles with geography in the
back of his mind, read:

"Hush. Be quiet. 'Tis Connecticut!"

It was a long while before Arthur heard the last of that
from the rest of the family. But the readings went on and
when Al finally caught up with the rest of the cast for the
dress rehearsal, he was perfect in his part.

News of the revival created interest not only in the old
parish but, because of the prominence of Smith, Walker,
Nolan, and others in the cast, all over town. So great was
the demand for tickets that the original plan to give only one
or two performances was abandoned and it was arranged that
the production should run for an entire week, which it did at
great profit to St. James's—and to no end of fun for the
members of the cast and their children. The latter, having
heard their fathers or mothers talk of the time in which they,
their faces smeared with grease paint, delighted audiences in
the old auditorium under the church, sat—now convulsed
with laughter, now entranced—as the footlights gleamed again
on the old stage and the years were turned back before their
eyes. The first appearance of Tom Nolan, who later was to become a justice of the Court of Special Sessions, caused his off-
spring to howl with glee, and there were snorts and chuckles
from the Smith children as Al, in a perfectly villainous role,
roared his threats at the handsome young hero who, in his
sailor suit of blue, retorted bravely.

From Broadway came the theatrical producers, and from
the newspaper offices the first-string drama critics, to view
this epic of the theater. And while it cannot be denied that
all of them had a thoroughly enjoyable time, it must be

admitted that none of them went back uptown sighing because the actors had sought other fields of endeavor, leaving the world of make-believe to its fate.

The spring of 1917 brought on this nation's entrance into World War I, and Al plunged into various patriotic activities which, indeed, took up more of his time than the duties of his office. There also devolved upon him that year the task of helping to plan a campaign by the Democrats that would unseat Mayor John Purroy Mitchel and result in the election of a Tammany candidate to the City Hall. Al didn't like the ultimate selection of Judge John F. Hylan, but he rode along with the party leaders and, to strengthen the ticket, agreed to run for the presidency of the Board of Aldermen.

Once more he had the endorsement of those factions that once were opposed to him, and, his own election being a foregone conclusion, he devoted most of his campaign speeches to the glory of Hylan, whom he privately considered incompetent. Thus, for what he considered the good of the party, and trusting that he and others in the administration could make up for Hylan's deficiencies, he quit the sheriff's office and, upon being elected, assumed control of the aldermen—or, at least, of their manners while they were in the aldermanic chamber. This being a legislative job, he liked it infinitely better than being sheriff, although the sheriff's office had not done badly by him: his salary and fees for two years had amounted roughly to $105,000.

He looked upon himself as a rich man now—he never would do so again, for never again would he net that much of a financial return from any position, with the tax scale rising from year to year. He never had had so fine a home, nor had been able to afford the summers he and his family now spent on Long Island. But his new-found riches did not blur in his mind the needs and problems of those who were poor, as he once had been. He ate regularly at Delmonico's and similar restaurants, but he didn't forget the fellow hunched on a stool in a lunchroom or coffee pot. He was driven about in automobiles—his own or one of the city's—but he looked after the interests of those who were packed into the subways. He looked with heartwarming pride on the benefits already being derived from the factory laws he had helped to create, and he sought unswervingly to increase those benefits.

He watched, carefully, over the spending of the city's money. There was, for instance, a secretarial post, established by law, in his office, and he filled it by the appointment of a young man who had served him briefly but well at Albany and whom he regarded as exceedingly promising. It paid $8,000 a year, and although it long had been looked upon as a political plum—that, indeed, was the reason for its creation—Al had the curious notion that anyone who filled it should earn his salary. His appointee, it seemed, had a different notion. He accepted the job as payment for services rendered in the past and spent as little time as possible in his office.

Busy with his new duties, Al didn't realize this at once. When he did, he called the young man to account.

"Listen," he said, "the taxpayers of New York aren't spending eight thousand dollars a year on you just to see your hat hanging in your office once in a while. You may not have an awful lot to do, but they expect you to do it. So do I. If I didn't, I would have picked somebody else for the job."

The young man promised to be more attentive to his duties thereafter, and for a few days made good on his promise. Then there was another lapse ... and another warning. The lapses became more frequent; the warnings still went unheeded. The few tasks that normally would have fallen to him were absorbed by others. A final warning having drawn no response from him, Smith went before the Board of Estimate and recommended that the job be abolished. Some of them shook their heads gravely over the thought of doing away with a job that meant $8,000 a year to one of the faithful, but they accepted his recommendation.

When, a day or so later, the young man sauntered in and hung up his hat, Al said:

"You can put that hat right on again and go where you please, son."

The young man was startled.

"Why?" he asked.

"Didn't you hear?" Al said. "You've been abolished."

There were times when, in Hylan's absence from the city— His Honor liked to play around Palm Beach or Miami when the wintry winds were blowing—Al acted as mayor. This experience gave him an insight into some of the intricacies of the city government, and from it he learned lessons that he would apply, one day, when he was governor, and that would be of great benefit to the city. This was a period in his life that has been all but forgotten except by those who were close to him at the time—a period in which, in the light of his later accomplishments, he almost seems to have been marking time, waiting for a summons to higher duties. Actually it was a period in which he not only served his city well but prepared himself, sometimes unknowingly, for the years that lay ahead of him.

Meanwhile, between the hours he spent at City Hall and in the various war activities which claimed him in constantly increasing numbers, there were happy times at 25 Oliver Street. The children—Alfred, Emily, Catherine, Arthur, and Walter—attended St. James's School, trudging up and down the same stairs that once had known the tread of his reluctant feet, sitting in the same classrooms where he had sat, sometimes so restlessly, going on Sundays to the church with their mother and father to receive Communion at the rail where he had knelt as a boy.

"I don't remember much of those days," Walter has said, "for I was only eight years old. But I do remember the big breakfasts we had and how my father would always insist on us eating well. He said that a good breakfast would carry a boy through the day.

"When I grew older, I realized that he ate a much bigger breakfast than anybody else I ever knew. When it had become the thing for most people to breakfast on fruit juice, toast, and coffee, he still would follow his fruit or fruit juice with such things as ham and eggs or—believe it or not—fried oysters or fried eels. And he would eat stacks of toast and drink three cups of hot coffee—and I mean hot. If it wasn't hot, you could hear him holler the length of the longest dining room you ever saw.

"I once asked him if he always had eaten breakfast like that, and he said no, because when he was a boy he couldn't afford them. He said he really started when he first went to Albany. Tom Caughlan, with whom he roomed then, was in the produce business and was so accustomed to getting up very early in the morning that he always would get up and go for a long walk before breakfast and then come back and eat the kind of breakfast he would have if he was still in the market. And so Father, eating with him every morning, got into the habit of eating as heavily. Even in those—for me—early Oliver Street days, I can remember such things as stewed or fried tripe and broiled chops or steak on the breakfast table."

13: THE MAN THEY WERE LOOKING FOR

THE CALL FOR WHICH HE HAD PREPARED HIM-self—consciously at times, and at others only by the acquisition of knowledge pertinent to the matter at hand and with no thought to his future—came sooner than he had expected. In August of 1918 he was designated to run in the primaries as the regular Democratic nominee for governor.

There was no dramatic prelude to his selection. While it is certain that by this time he very definitely was thinking of himself as gubernatorial timber, there were those higher in the party's councils who, while inclined to think of him that way, too, were of the opinion that he was not ready for advancement to the highest office in the state. The opening for him was made by chance, as a matter of fact.

There was abroad in the state at the time a general feeling, which inspired optimism in the Democrats and marked apprehension in the Republicans, that Governor Whitman could not be re-elected. The general complaint was that Whitman, in his second term, had kept only one eye on the affairs of the state while the other roamed toward Washington, and that the buzzing of a presidential bee in his bonnet distracted his attention from the voices of the people he had sworn to serve. As summer came on, his defeat seemed so sure to the Democrats that they felt almost any sound candidate they picked would triumph in November.

Murphy, still absolute boss of Tammany Hall, and, in view of the Hall's unimpaired power, virtually boss of the entire state machine, began looking about him for a suitable standard-bearer. Al was not Murphy's first choice, any more than, in the beginning, he had been Tom Foley's first choice for the Assembly. It seemed to Murphy that, with a huge New York City plurality waiting to be plucked by anyone he might name, it was chiefly important to call up a candidate from one of the northern counties who could harvest the upstate vote.

To this end, a meeting of Murphy and the lesser bosses was held at the Syracuse home of William F. Kelly, the leader of Onondaga County, at which the qualifications of a number of men were discussed. Three days of argument, even wrangling, having failed to bring forth a suitable candidate, the meeting adjourned to New York. There, too, the quest for a standout candidate was fruitless. The conclusion reached was that a man put up by the Hall would pass muster if his selection could be engineered in such a manner that it could be made to appear it was the work of the upstate leaders at a conference to be held in Saratoga shortly thereafter.

It was at this conference, or sort of unofficial convention, that Smith's name was presented along with some twenty others. Al, who was present, was in a spot where he could do nothing to push his own candidacy; but, it soon developed, no help from any quarter was needed to put him over. As the potential candidates were considered, one by one ... and their names were struck from the list, one by one ... his name loomed larger in the minds of the leaders. They discovered, almost overnight, that the man they had sought so earnestly from one end of the state to the other had been in their midst all the time. At the end of three days of deliberation, he was their unanimous choice. First word of his selection was relayed to Oliver Street by Arthur, then eleven years old. The boy had been taken to Saratoga by his father's friend Tom Campbell, and as soon as he heard the news he rushed to a telephone and called his mother.

Many elements of the population of New York City other than those identified with Tammany Hall enthusiastically supported the Democratic nominee. Among them was a group of Democrats, Republicans, and independent voters who formed a citizens' committee headed by Abram Elkus (he had served as counsel of the Factory Commission) and opened headquarters at the Hotel Biltmore.

With the formation of this committee there came into Smith's sphere a woman whose influence on him and on his political future would be tremendous. Through the years that would follow, she would be at his side, guiding, suggesting, urging, restraining him, helping to mold him into a great public figure, and he would rely implicitly on her judgment in matters that would affect every resident of the state. Did she, in the early days of the committee, vision the place she would fill in the coming years? Perhaps. She already had dedicated her services to him beyond her duties as chairman of the women's division, and she was farseeing and strong-willed and it may have been that even then she sensed not only his destiny but the part she was to play in working it out. Her name was Belle Moskowitz.

Belle Moskowitz was then in her forty-first year. Beautiful in her youth, she was now an extremely attractive woman. Her parents were Isidor and Esther Lindner, and she was born on October 5, 1877, in a small flat over her father's watchmaking shop at One Hundred and Twenty-sixth Street and Third Avenue. Having been graduated from grade school and the Horace Mann High School, she enrolled in Teachers College at Columbia University, where she specialized in literature, psychology, logic, and languages. Passionately devoted to helping the underprivileged, she plunged into social work at eighteen, and as a result of a presentation by the Boys' Club of the Educational Alliance at East Broadway and Jefferson Street of a play she wrote and directed—it was her own version of Mark Twain's *Puddin' Head Wilson*—she was appointed director of entertainments and exhibits at the Alliance, with a salary of $500 a year.

Among the friends she made in the course of her work were Charles M. Israels, a nephew of the Dutch painter Joseph

Israels, and a leader of the Boys' Club at the Alliance; and Henry Moskowitz of the Madison Street Settlement House near by—the same Henry Moskowitz who had enlisted Al's aid after the Triangle fire. On November 11, 1903, she married Israels, to whom she bore three children, Josef, Carlos, and Miriam. Israels died in 1911, and, left with three small children, the widow struggled on, working hard to support them.

Meanwhile she was becoming a vital factor in settlement work, and, to the degree that it affected social legislation, she became interested in politics. She was for a long time violently anti-Tammany, notably clashing with some of the Tammany-inspired regulations covering (too loosely, she thought) the East Side dance halls where some of her charges among young girls sought relaxation.

In November of 1914 she was married again, this time to Moskowitz, a graduate of the University of Erlangen, Germany, with a degree in philosophy. She continued her social work, with added emphasis on the care and guidance of girls, and, as one phase of her campaign, helped Grace Dodge to form the Travelers' Aid Society.

She had been attracted to Smith's ceaseless sponsorship of social legislation, and this had won her support of the Democratic party. She saw in him a new hope for the people she championed, and when he was nominated for governor she asked her friend Judge Elkus to allow her to join his staff.

One day, as the campaign got under way, she asked Smith if he would address a meeting of the Women's University Club, to be held at the Cosmopolitan Club a week hence. She was a member of the club, she explained.

He was loath to accept, at first, never having spoken before to a group composed solely of women, but she persuaded him to do so. His speech was one of the best he made during the campaign and one of the best he ever made. It is memorable because, in the course of it, he pronounced his political credo:

"I know what is right. If I ever do anything that is wrong, it will not be because I don't know it to be so and you can mark it down as being willful and deliberate and hold me to account for it."

No man running for public office ever had put himself so squarely on the spot as he had with those words. No man ever more forcefully impressed his hearers with his sincerity.

14: VICTORY: THE NEW GOVERNOR

THE CAMPAIGN WAS AN ARDUOUS ONE. THE war was rolling to its violent close, and in France, New York's Twenty-seventh Division was smashing at the Hindenburg line, breaking the backbone of German resistance. At home an epidemic of influenza was raging through cities and military concentrations, taking a heavy toll of life and bringing about a quarantine of many public gathering places. Newspaper space was given grudgingly to Smith and Whitman, and many of the meetings they were scheduled to address either were called off or but lightly attended. This, of course, favored Whitman, who was waging a purely defensive fight from the vantage point of the governor's office, and imposed severe restrictions on the challenger, who had to hurl his blasts from any angle.

Although the situation, right from the beginning, presaged a closer fight than Murphy and the other Democratic leaders had anticipated, Al met it wisely and forcefully. He had the backing of some of the state's most substantial people, as reflected in the make-up of the Citizens' Committee; the advice of able leaders; and in his own right, a broad experience in the affairs of the state, an alert mind, a ready wit, and, quite important in those pre-radio campaigns, a loud voice. He learned, too, that the impression he had made when touring the state as vice-chairman of the Factory Commission had endured. He was not a stranger asking for votes in the upstate cities and towns. He was the one who had combed those communities for facts upon which he had fashioned legislation that had benefited the workers throughout the state, and in general he was well received. The Anti-Saloon League heaped abuse on him, tying him up with the liquor interests in its propaganda, and in some of the rural counties he was condemned because of his religion, but neither the bluenoses nor the bigots were as yet strong enough to defeat him as they would be one day in a greater, more important fight.

Whitman, unnerved, perhaps, by the specter of defeat that haunted him, played straight into Al's hands with some ill-considered and totally unjust remarks. On one occasion he laid himself wide open to a haymaker from the challenger by calling attention to the many years Al had held public office, winding up with the silly crack:

"He never earned a dollar with his hands."

Al promptly flattened him with a sentence:

"When my opponent was a student at Amherst," he said, "I was working from dawn till dark in the Fulton Fish Market."

The campaign reached a terrific climax on election day. A delay in returns from that section of the state centering in Syracuse had everybody at the Democratic headquarters in the Biltmore worried, for it had seemed that, close as the voting was, Smith was a certain winner. Suspecting that all was not right in the region that, inexplicably, had been blacked out, Smith, Bob Wagner, Jimmy Walker, and Alfred Johnson rushed to Syracuse on Wednesday morning and there, with the aid of the local committee, checked up on the voting. Satisfied by Thursday that Al had gained a majority, the group returned to New York where, to their joy, they learned that with the aid of the soldier vote in the camps in the United States, he had won by about 15,000.

Whitman, however, was far from satisfied. He charged that skullduggery had been committed by Tammany Hall in districts of New York City and insisted that the ballot boxes in the suspected districts be opened. This was done, and when a recount failed to reveal any irregularities, he at length ... and not too graciously ... conceded his defeat and congratulated the victor.

There were two other interesting developments of this election. One was that Al's mother and wife, who had shared his old predjudice against woman suffrage, had repented and cast their first votes for him. The second was that in Al's own district, two votes had been counted for Whitman. Some of the boys thought perhaps a floater hired by the Republicans not only had sneaked in but, in some manner, had managed to repeat. Al, amused, asked the district captain for an explanation.

Embarrassed, angered, the captain said:

"I don't know yet who voted against you, Al. But I'll find out if it is the last thing I do."

By whatever means he employed, he got the information within three days. One vote had been cast by a man who believed Al could have wangled an appointment to the police force for his son, and didn't. The other was a sorry mistake. A woman, who lived on Cherry Street and had been a schoolmate of Al's, had been confused by the symbols at the top of the ballot—this having been her first visit to the polls—and had put her mark under the Republican eagle instead of the Democratic star.

Whitman's contest of the election, short-lived though it was, delayed official confirmation of Smith's victory. It was not until very near the end of December that Al received his certificate of election from the secretary of state. By that time he had composed his first message to the legislature and the Smith family had packed its bags for the trip to Albany.

It was on December 30, 1918, that Al, Mrs. Smith, his mother, and the children entered the Executive Mansion, there to celebrate with a few friends in the great dining hall the forty-fifth birthday of the Governor-elect. Presiding over the serving of the dinner was Harry Whitehead, major-domo of the mansion. Harry had taken an immediate liking to this new family and, being fond of children, his eyes were lighted and his smile wide as he looked at the boys and girls gathered about the table.

Oliver Street ... and Catherine, Madison, Pearl, Dover, Cherry, and all the streets round about ... moved to Albany for the inauguration, leaving behind only the very old, the very young, and those who couldn't dig up the price of a round-trip ticket. Albany never had seen anything quite like it, nor ever will again in all likelihood, for Al's subsequent inaugurations were pale by comparison.

This was the one, this first swearing in of the boy who had used the Downtown Tammany Club as a springboard to the greatest honor the state of New York could confer on one of its sons, and everybody wanted to be there to see it. The usual crowd that swarms into Albany to see a governor—any governor—take office was there, of course. But the influx from the East Side swirled about it, engulfed it, finally closed over it. On the night before, the hotels bulged and still the trains arriving from New York disgorged thousands who, too excited to sleep, tramped the streets or jammed the all-night restaurants—and all the restaurants in Albany stayed open all that night.

Hummed, whistled, sung, roared on the night air, old songs of New York rolled over the town. Wake up, Albany! Here we are! Make room for us! We're here to see Al! Our boy, our guy! The guy from South Street and the Fulton Fish Market and Oliver Street! The guy in the brown derby! The Governor! Going to be the greatest governor the state ever had!

And, in the Executive Mansion, the Governor-to-be sitting with Katie and his mother ... and Emily and Catherine and Al and Arthur and Walter and his friends. Laughing, talking, turning to Tom Foley, looking fondly at his wife and children, patting his aging mother's hand, musing on the days of long ago. The days when he ran the streets and swam in the river. The cold, gray mornings when he walked past the

The Smith Family on the Steps of 25 Oliver Street about 1915

Al Smith with Al Smith, Jr., Emily Warner, Major Warner and Two
Grandchildren

Fishing and Golfing Were Two Favorite Forms of Relaxation

silent, sleep-filled houses on Cherry Street on his way to serve at six o'clock mass at St. James's. The long, hard days in the fish market. The nights when he journeyed by elevated railroad and trolley car to the distant Bronx to call on pretty Catherine Dunn. The night that ... was it only fourteen years ago? ... he and Tom Caughlan arrived in Albany and stayed awake till dawn, fearing the old Keeler Hotel would burn down and they would be trapped in their beds. (It hadn't been such a bad hunch, at that. The Keeler did burn down one night!)

Thinking of the night he had gone to the governor's reception, right here in this very house, and had been ushered in and out so fast it had made his head swim. And of how he had come away saying:

"If I ever become governor..."

Well, he was governor now, or would be when he took the oath of office on the morrow. He had come a long way and he had worked hard and been faithful to the trust that his party had reposed in him. He had served the people well and they had rewarded him and ...

He glanced across the room to where his wife sat, with Emily and Catherine by her side, and she saw him looking at her and smiled.

On inaugural day the Sixty-ninth Regiment of the National Guard—New York's Fighting Sixty-ninth that had smashed its way across France as a unit of the famed Rainbow Division—led the parade. The crowd, packed along the line of march, broke as the parade passed and ran to cluster about the steps of the Capitol where, his voice trembling with the emotion that surged through him, the new governor took the oath.

"I solemnly swear ..."

Cannon boomed on Capitol Hill at the completion of the ceremony, and the crowd, which had been silent, roared its tribute to the man whose fortunes it had followed from the sidewalks of New York to the top of the broad steps on which he stood so proudly, and yet so humbly, now.

That night, at the inaugural ball, Oliver Street . . . and all the streets round about . . . met the new neighbors from the north, from the Hudson Valley to the Canadian border. And among the guests were Tom Foley and Charles F. Murphy, come to share the happiness of him whose political destiny they had guarded so well.

A few nights later Al held his reception for the members of the legislature. He had not forgotten the promise he had made to himself fourteen years before. In spite of the loud squawks of the perennial invitation grabbers and gate crashers, only senators and assemblymen and their families gained entrance to the mansion, and everybody had the pleasant time he had hoped to have the night he wore white tie and tails for the first time.

15: THE GOVERNOR AT WORK

NOW THE PARADES, THE RECEPTIONS, AND the dances were over. The sound of cannon fire had died away and the crowd had dispersed to Syracuse and Rochester and Buffalo and all the towns between and beyond, to Oliver Street and Madison and Catherine and the Bowery. In his office in the Capitol or sometimes late at night in his study in the mansion, the new governor was grappling with the problems that assailed him.

To help him he had his secretary, and already an old friend, George R. Van Namee. Van Namee was a lawyer from Watertown and the Democratic chairman of Jefferson County. He had come to Albany to stay for a long time—although he did not realize it then—on the election of Governor Dix in 1910.

"We Democrats in Jefferson County didn't know what patronage was, up to that time," he once recounted, "because we never had a chance to exercise it or derive any benefits from it. We were entirely surrounded by Republicans, who won all the offices and held all the jobs, and since being Democrats never did us any good, people thought we were that way just out of pure cussedness. But when that Democratic sweep came, we were notified that we could have three jobs at Albany. One of them was that of assistant clerk of the assembly, which paid $3,500 a year, and being the county chairman and having the first pick, I picked that one.

"I didn't have any intention of staying there long. I had a law practice that was coming along nicely and had no desire to leave Watertown permanently, but this seemed like a good

chance to spend a few months in Albany, meet a lot of people
I had heard about, get myself known a little bit where it
might help me in my practice later on, and, in the bargain,
get paid for the experience."

It didn't work out the way he had planned. Luke Mc-
Henry, the clerk of the assembly, was in poor health, and
almost from the beginning the newcomer from the north
assumed most of McHenry's duties.

"The first time I was ever in the Assembly chamber," he
said, "I called the roll on a bill."

He knew Al Smith but only slightly, having met him at a
party in the home of a mutual friend two years before.

"He was very slim then, looked a lot like his son Al did
when he was just springing up."

As acting clerk, and following his promotion to the top
post on McHenry's death, Van Namee worked closely with
Smith as majority leader and, later, as speaker. Soon they
were firm friends and they were to remain so as long as Al
lived, and George was to be of great help to Al in years to
come as secretary, member of the Public Service Commission,
and state Democratic chairman.

They were hard at it now, for these were restless times,
coming in the wake of the war, and notations in Van Namee's
carefully kept yearbook for 1919 prove they seldom quit work
until one or two o'clock in the morning. New legislation,
some of it strange in character, was presented, debated,
passed, and sent to him for the Governor's signature. State
ratification of the new amendments to the United States Constitution providing for woman suffrage and Prohibition...
bills aimed at the ousting from the Assembly of five Socialists
just elected from New York ... bills that would have given
the Appellate Court the power of life and death over political
parties. There were reforms the Governor had in mind that
could not be worked out because of the antiquated design of
the state departments. There were the usual number of seemingly unimportant and innocuous bills which, had they been

carelessly signed, would have been virtual licenses to steal for those who had inspired them. These last were disposed of as swiftly as they reached the Governor's desk. Having vetoed one of them, he said to Van Namee:

"Remember this one? I fought against it and defeated it six years ago. But bills like this keep coming back. I'll probably see it again sometime."

Following the practice he had begun in the days when he was a neophyte and which he had continued through all his service as an assemblyman, he read every bill throughly, line for line and word for word, and with that memory for which he was becoming famous, retained every word of it. During a hearing on one voluminous bill, the senator who had introduced it said:

"This bill provides..."

"Where does it say that?" Al demanded.

"It's in there, all right," the senator said.

Smith had a copy of the bill before him. Picking it up, he handed it to the senator.

"Show me where," he said.

The senator, his embarrassment increasing as he turned each page in search of the passage, said at length:

"I am unable to find it, although I was sure I had covered that point."

When the hearing was over, a reporter asked Al how he knew the disputed passage was missing.

"I read the bill last night," he said.

"Even so," the reporter said, "how could you practically memorize a bill of that length?"

Al grinned at him.

"Maybe," he said, "it is because my mind never was cluttered up by an education."

The legislature was in the tight grip of Republicans. Many of them were Al's personal friends, who dined with him at the mansion or accompanied him on trips to New York, and on many occasions showed their liking for him. Politically, however, they were his implacable enemies and fought every measure he proposed, regardless of its merits. Added to their opposition was an attitude that annoyed him even more than their tactics in the frequent stand-up fights between them.

"They act as though they thought I got here by accident," he said. "They seem to think that I don't carry any weight and that when my term is over, I will be thrown out of the Capitol and never heard from again."

He reacted to their hostility, with its accompanying superciliousness, in the only way he knew: he fought back savagely, demonstrating that if his opponents did not take him seriously as governor, he took himself and the affairs of the state very seriously indeed. He stoutly defended the Socialists under fire, although he had no sympathy with the principles of the Socialist party. He denounced aspersions cast on the loyalty of the schoolteachers by bills demanding that they take an oath of allegiance to the nation. He combated bills that threatened the integrity of the schools, public and private alike. He was outspoken against Prohibition and warmly receptive to ratification of woman suffrage, although once he had been opposed to it.

He selected the heads of state departments carefully and without consideration as to their political affiliations, several of his appointees having none whatever. In his opening message he advocated the abolition of the State Police Department, which had been established two years before, but after discussing that body with its founder and superintendent, Colonel George L. Chandler, a physician from Kingston, he quickly recognized its worth and, admitting his mistake, declared his wholehearted support of it. Strikes were frequent as a reflection of the unsettled labor conditions following the war, but he settled them either in person or through the offices of Miss Frances Perkins, whom he had appointed a member of the State Industrial Commission. Bitterly assailed by William Randolph Hearst, the publisher, for having allegedly been responsible for a rise in the price of milk in New York City, he lashed back so violently as to cause the publisher to withdraw from the fight.

One of the most important of his undertakings was the organization of the Reconstruction Committee. This was suggested by Mrs. Moskowitz, who, as keen a student of public affairs as he was, urged that a competent body be chosen to study the make-up of the state's machinery of government and report on desired changes. This, when organized, was composed of representatives of capital and labor, large businesses and small, banking, insurance, law, science, agriculture, and social service. Abram Elkus was elected chairman, and Mrs. Moskowitz secretary. The study mapped out for it included state departments, taxation and financing, and all the human needs of the population, with special emphasis on housing.

The commission, created in January of 1919, elicited only scorn from the legislative leaders, who dubbed it a "rump legislature" and refused to appropriate money to finance its operations. In spite of this and with the encouragement of Smith and some farseeing Republicans, such as Charles Evans Hughes, John Lord O'Brian, and Marin Saxe, the commission went ahead with its work, supported by private contributions, many of which were made by members of the commission.

With all the harassment to which he was subjected, Smith thrived and gained in power and stature . . . and took time out for evenings at home or occasional trips through the state, when as often as possible he was accompanied by Mrs. Smith and the chidren and as many friends as he could collect. One who was a frequent house guest at the mansion and went on many of the trips was—remember Mamie Leary, the belle of Oliver Street in her youth and a star of the St. James Players? Now Mrs. Thomas Collins, widow of a race-track figure, she was Mrs. Smith's closest friend, and a frequent house guest at the mansion.

The children found the mansion and the grounds wonderful places in which to play, and Al shared their delight in a zoo which they had established in the rear of the house. It was inhabited by goats, deer, and a few small animals the children had collected here and there or that had been given to them. Lording it over all the other animals, however, was Caesar, a Great Dane, whom Al had had for a number of years and who soon became as well known in Albany as he had been in Oliver Street. Al was fond of repeating one story about Caesar, which dated from the night of the family's arrival in Albany. As the Smiths entered the mansion, he was taken off the leash on which Arthur had led him up from the station—or vice versa—and bounded into the main hall, giving a great scare to Governor Whitman, who was waiting to receive his successor in office.

"What's that?" the startled Governor exclaimed at sight of the huge and ferocious-looking—but entirely harmless—Caesar.

"Haw!" Al roared. "That's the Tammany Tiger come up to take over Albany!"

The first Christmas was a memorable one. The year before, the family had been cooped up in a suite at the Biltmore and Al had been so busy with his first message and other details of the work that lay ahead of him, and the children so excited about going to Albany, that Christmas had sort of sneaked up on all of them. But in 1919 there had been plenty of time in which to prepare for it—and what a place in which to celebrate it!

"This is like Christmas on Oliver Street," young Al said. And added: "Only more so."

It scarcely could have been better. Gifts for the family poured in from all over the state, some of them from people they scarcely knew or never had heard of, while none of them ever had seen a tree such as that which stood in the great parlor and under which the gifts were piled high on Christmas Eve. Al's mother came up from Brooklyn, and as the Governor looked at her in these surroundings, with the lights twinkling on the tree and the logs blazing in the fireplace, he could not help but think of some of the Christmases they had known when he was a boy and times had been so hard.

On his regular week-end visits to New York, he did not neglect the Downtown Tammany Club but spent as much time there as he had when he was an assemblyman. He also tried appearing every Saturday morning in the Governor's Room at the City Hall to listen to complaints, suggestions, and pleas of all sorts from the citizens of the town, but he had to abandon this practice, worth while as he believed it to be, for the room never was large enough to hold all those who wished to see him nor the time at his disposal long enough to listen to them. Besides, he discovered that most of those who called on him either wanted jobs or sought his help in straightening out some matter over which he had no control.

But around the Downtown Tammany Club it was as it always had been: the neighbors coming and going, looking for jobs, district captains making reports, hangers-on playing cards, the air thick with tobacco smoke. And, as always, Tom Foley at his desk, listening attentively to everything that was said, giving orders, advice, putting his hand in his pocket now and then in answer to a call for help from one he knew deserved it. Smith, now governor, was as much a part of the scene as he always had been, laughing, telling stories.

Very often he was accompanied by Van Namee, who, as a self-tagged country boy, was seeing this side of big-town political life for the first time. Once, when a seeker of favor from the Governor departed disgruntled because whatever it was he wanted was not within the Governor's power to grant him, Al said:

"He reminds me of a fellow who came in here one night when I was an assemblyman. He wanted a job as an elevator operator in the Municipal Building and I said:

"'Why, I can't do anything about that. That's a civil service job.'

"He huffed around for a while and then he said:

"'Christy Sullivan could get it for me.'

"So I said: 'Well, why don't you go see Christy Sullivan, then?'

"And he said: 'I've tried to see him but I can't find him.'

"'How many times did you try?' I asked him.

"'Three times,' he said, 'but I can't find him.'

"I didn't say anything and he went out, still sore at me. In other words I—whom he had no trouble in seeing, and I'd have been glad to help him, if I could—was a so-and-so for not getting the job for him, while Christy Sullivan, who plainly was ducking him, was a great fellow."

On another night, when Van Namee was there, two Italians came in, one carrying a clothing box under his arm.

"Good evening, Mr. Foley," the one with the box said. Then he looked at the Governor.

"Hello, Al," he said.

He turned again to Foley.

"Mr. Foley," he said, "I am a tailor and I made this suit for this man."

He untied the string on the box, took the suit out and held it up.

"He claims it don't fit him but I say it does. We want you to decide who is right."

Foley laughed.

"How about letting the Governor decide?" he said.

"O. K. with me," the tailor said.

He turned to the customer.

"O. K. with you?"

The customer nodded.

"All right. Put the suit on and let Al look at you."

They went into the meeting room, where there was a raised platform at one end, and the customer, having put on the suit, climbed on the platform. Al had him turn this way and that.

"The coat should be lifted under the arms," he said to the tailor, "and the pants are too long."

"O.K.," the tailor said.

"Take it off," he said to the customer.

He put the suit back in the box and when the customer had put his old suit on, they started for the door.

"Good night, Mr. Foley," the tailor said.

The customer, who hadn't said a word, turned and smiled at the Governor.

"Thanks, Al," he said.

When they had gone, Van Namee shook his head.

"The folks in Jefferson County wouldn't believe it," he said.

16: PROGRESS—AND A GALLING DEFEAT

THE YEAR 1920 WAS AN EVENTFUL ONE FOR Smith. In it he was to add to his reputation as administrator of the state's business, to hear himself nominated for the presidency of the United States—and to be rejected at the polls when he sought re-election in November.

Legislative opposition to his plans, strong as it had been in 1919, was even stronger as the new year unwound. In spite of it, he justifiably felt his record was such as to entitle him to two years more in which to complete the reforms he had begun and which constantly were being suggested by the reports of the Reconstruction Commission. He was to be caught up, however, by the wave of revulsion against all things Democratic that swept the country that year, and it would carry him out of Albany.

Meanwhile, there was the Democratic national convention, which was held in San Francisco. Al had been to national conventions before, but this one promised to be—and was, so far as he was concerned—more exciting than any of the others. Moreover, he never had been to the Pacific coast, and the trip across the country was fascinating in itself. With him went his wife, young Al, Emily, Charles F. Murphy and his wife, Judge James A. Foley and his wife, General Charles W. Berry, and William Humphreys. The convention resulted in the nomination of James M. Cox, but before this, Al, hiding in the rear of the hall, listened, thrilled, to the only notable speech of the week, that in which Bourke Cockran extolled him as New York's candidate for President. Cockran, one of the great orators of the old school and long the golden voice of Tammany, told him the night before:

"I am about to achieve the joy of my life. For as long as I can remember, I have been fanning the breeze against somebody or something. This time I will be for somebody."

It was a great speech, but it didn't mean anything and no one knew this better than Al. He knew that Murphy had sent his name to the convention only to see what reaction, if any, it would have; and it had none, at least immediately. At the end of the speech, the New York delegates cheered and the band flung itself into a song that, forever after, would be identified with the name of Al Smith:

"East Side, West Side, all around the town,
"The tots sang 'Ring a' rosy, London Bridge is
          falling down....'"

It was the first time it ever had been played for him. The age-old custom at conventions was for the band to play the state song for every favorite son nominated, but no one could think of the state song of New York or even if the state had one, and in desperation the leader of this band came up with "East Side, West Side." It is curious that the playing of it on that occasion should have been so much a matter of chance, not at all curious that it should have been associated with the very mention of him all the rest of his life. For the song is as much a part of New York as any stick or stone that goes to make up the town ... and surely the town never had another citizen who was as much a part of its throbbing life.

The cheers and the music died away, and, after a brief pause, the nominations were resumed. Respected and popular though he was in New York, Al was little known throughout the rest of the country at that time, and to a majority of the delegates from states other than New York he was just another local hero to be dutifully and politely cheered for a few minutes and then passed over.

And yet it had been shrewd on Murphy's part to have his

name put before the convention. Al wasn't ready yet...but there would be other years and other conventions, and this was a part of the grooming Murphy was giving him. For Murphy, silent, thoughtful, always alert, always with his eyes on the young men of his party, had been watching every step of Al's progress at Albany. He was convinced that there would be a day when Al Smith, introduced at a convention, would be rewarded with more than the tooting of horns, the blaring of a carefully coached band, and the cheers of a well-organized claque.

To top off the convention and for relaxation before heading back to New York and the gubernatorial campaign that already was shaping up, Al and his family visited Los Angeles and, of course, Hollywood. They toured the motion picture studios and were photographed with many of the stars, swam in the Pacific Ocean off Catalina Island, and on the way back to New York stopped off at Denver and ascended Pike's Peak in an automobile.

Al's nomination for re-election as governor was a foregone conclusion. As his Republican opponent, he drew the frosty Nathan L. Miller. It was a curiously jumbled campaign that they waged, with Al trying to keep before the voters the things he had done and the things he hoped to do, and hammering away at the worth of the Reconstruction Commission; but for all the good it did him, he might as well have saved his breath. Miller, taking his cue from the Republican national platform, confined himself to the League of Nations and other questions agitating the country as a whole as an aftermath of the war. That, apparently, was all anyone cared to listen to.

That Al sensed what lay in store for him was indicated in his comment to Mrs. Smith on the eve of the election.

"I am afraid," he said, "that tomorrow night will be no night for getting out the brooms."

He was referring to an old custom in the Second District: On receiving news of his repeated elections to the Assembly by overwhelming majorities, the neighbors on Oliver Street would thrust brooms out the windows of their homes to indicate a clean sweep.

Mrs. Smith, nurtured on her husband's victories, did not share his apprehension.

"Oh, yes, it will," she said. "The brooms will be there as usual."

But he was right. Warren G. Harding defeated Cox for the presidency, and Miller, riding on his coat tails, went into office with him, although Al ran far ahead of the other members of the Democratic ticket. He had, too, this consolation: Of the sixty-two Assembly districts in New York City, Harding failed to carry only one. That was the Second. Oliver Street . . . and Catherine and Madison and the others in the old Fourth Ward . . . had been faithful.

It was late on election night and Al Smith was very low. Seven years later he would know a more crushing defeat than that which he had just suffered, and when it came he would be deeply saddened, not because a great honor had been denied him but because the denial would indicate a national state of mind that to him, as to millions of others, would be no less than tragic. But now, as he sat in the headquarters at the Biltmore, where the last, straggling, unimportant votes were being tabulated—unimportant because the issue long since had been decided—he was overcome by a sense of frustration.

It was the frustration of a fighter called beaten by a judge who had not bothered to count the punches he had thrown. Aware, from the beginning, of the strength of the forces running against him, he had fought more skillfully and vigorously than ever before. His tactics had been sound and the blows he had hurled had been well timed, and yet it had been almost as though no one were looking—or listening. All he had achieved at Albany and all he hoped to achieve had, in his own words, run for Sweeney. Intent upon the old American custom of turning the rascals out, the voters had turned him out with them.

His first impulse, which did not die easily, was to foreswear politics, at least to the extent of never running for office again. Let somebody else hold the bag from there on. He might advise them, if asked to do so, how best to hold it to avoid being stuck with it, but he would not hold it himself, ever again. Virtually all his adult life had been spent in service to the people of his district, his county, his city, and his state. And today the people hadn't been able to get to the polls fast enough to show him the way to go home.

Home? Oliver Street. That was home. He would take Mrs. Smith and the children back to Oliver Street and they would stay there and be happy. There would be opportunities—any number of them, he knew—to go into business, and he would take one of them and settle down and the people could look to someone else to fight their battles for them. He would always have their interests at heart, he knew, even in this hour of frustration, and if they wanted any help from him he would give it to them, shabbily though he felt they had treated him. But not to the extent of going back to Albany— or anywhere else—and sweating out their problems.

In his bitterness he felt not even the slightest resentment toward the man who had defeated him. He and Nathan Miller were about as unlike as two men could be, save that each was honest and had a sincere desire to run the state government as ably as he could. Yet these two men, so unlike in person and differing so widely in politics, had great respect and admiration for each other and were genuinely cordial when they met.

Feeling as he did toward Miller, Al not only was quick to congratulate him on his victory but assured him of his willingness to help him in any way possible to an understanding of some of the little-known problems confronting a new governor on taking office. He added that he would be more than pleased to have Miller call on him at Albany at Miller's convenience, so that they might go over together any matters that the Governor-elect had in mind.

Not without its humorous angle is the circumstance that when Miller accepted the invitation, it very nearly disrupted Al's relations with the oldest and best friend he had—Tom Foley. Al and Miller were deep in conversation when a secretary came in with word that Foley had just arrived. Al merely nodded, thinking that Foley would not care to take part in or even listen to the conversation—in which assumption he was correct—and went right on talking to Miller. The meeting lasted longer than he had thought, and on walking to the door with Miller, he saw no sign of Foley.

"Where's Mr. Foley?" he asked the secretary.

"He's gone. He said he waited long enough."

"Gone? Where?"

"He didn't say."

"Telephone around and see if you can find him," Al said.

Foley, although many, not knowing him well, would not have suspected it, was very sensitive, especially where Smith was concerned. This had led to small quarrels between them before and—although the affection between them always would be almost that of a father and son—would lead to others. But this, Al sensed, was serious, and his fears were confirmed when he learned that Tom had left for New York.

He called a mutual friend on the telephone in New York and explained what had happened.

"Meet Tom at the train and square me with him," he said.

Al could almost see his friend shrug over the telephone.

"You know Tom," the friend said. "The only one who can square you with him is yourself. Call him up tonight, or, if you're coming down tomorrow, go see him and straighten it out."

"I'm going down," Al said. "I'll see him."

It required a little talking on his part, at that, to thaw Foley out the following day. Tom, feeling that Al had brushed him off because Miller was in the office, hadn't liked the look of it and said so very plainly. Now Al was aggrieved.

"You should have known better than that, Tom," he said.

Foley smiled.

"I guess you're right, Al," he said. "Let's forget about it."

The cordial relations between Smith and Miller were heightened a few nights later. Mrs. Smith, extending the customary invitation of the retiring governor's wife to show the wife of the governor-elect through the mansion and explain to her how the household is managed, added an invitation to dinner, which was accepted. Al then called Miller on the telephone.

"What kind of party would you like to have?" he asked. "Shall we have some guests in, or do you want just the family?"

"Just the family," Miller said. "I think that would be fine."

And so the Smith family met the Millers and liked them very much. This came as something of a surprise to Arthur and Walter, who had been prepared to dislike the man who had defeated their father. He already had been the cause of considerable heckling of them on the part of their schoolmates. On election night Emily, in New York with her mother, had thought of the younger boys at home in Albany and had said:

"Don't you think I should call Arthur and Walter and tell them?"

"Yes," her mother said.

Arthur answered the telephone. He sounded very glum.

"Yeah, we know," he said. Then: "Hey! Do we have to go to school tomorrow?"

"I suppose so. Why?"

"Aw, the kids will be laying for us to kid us about Pop getting licked. Ask Mother if we can stay home."

Emily laughed.

"You might just as well go," she said. "They'll be laying for you just the same the next day."

So Arthur and Walter decided to get it over with as quickly as possible and went to school the following day. Their fears had not been groundless. Crepe was hung on a picture of Al in Arthur's classroom. On a blackboard in Walter's room, a boy had scribbled:

"Three cheers for Miller!"

In the playground, boys yelled at them:

"Your old man got licked! Your old man got licked!"

Small wonder they—to put it mildly—didn't like Miller. But that dinner served to change their minds about him. They discovered that while he may have lacked something of their father's jovial disposition, he was a nice guy.

Now, as December waned, the family had to pack up, pull stakes, and go back to Oliver Street. The small excitements of life in the mansion were over. The zoo was broken up and the animals, save for the dogs, given away. There was a Christmas party, their last in the mansion, forever, they thought . . . and during Christmas week, the retreat of the children to New York while Al and Mrs. Smith remained in Albany to welcome the new governor and his wife and to attend his inauguration.

"I'm leaving, too, as soon as I get the Millers settled," Harry Whitehead said.

"You're leaving?" Mrs. Smith asked, surprised. "Why?"

Harry shook his head.

"It isn't going to be the same around here when you folks leave," he said.

17: BACK HOME ON OLIVER STREET

THE HOUSE ON OLIVER STREET SEEMED SOME-what cramped to the Smiths after two years in the mansion, but it had been entirely refurbished and was bright and inviting, and there was a white-jacketed Negro butler who was at once the wonder and the envy of the neighbors. Once the resettlement had been completed, the children went off to boarding school, and at dinner the first night after they had gone, Al looked across the table and, smiling, said to his wife:

"Well, Katy, we're right back where we started. Just the two of us sitting down to dinner."

But there was no heartiness in his smile, nor in that with which his wife answered it. The house was depressingly quiet and they were very lonely and ate almost in silence. There were no more references to the children that night nor in the morning—but when Al returned from the office, there were Arthur and Walter, the two youngest children, to greet him. Their mother, without a word to him, had taken them out of boarding school.

Meanwhile, Al had made his choice of the business opportunities that had been offered to him. These had been numerous, but after careful deliberation he had selected that which had come to him first. Immediately after the election he had gone to French Lick, Indiana, for a rest, and there he had met Fred Upham, of Chicago, at that time treasurer of the Republican National Committee, and George Getz, who was an associate of his in business, and they had offered him the presidency of the United States Trucking Corporation in New York City at a salary of $50,000.

There was a sentimental slant to the offer that attracted him (the $50,000 a year wasn't so bad, after two years in Albany at only $10,000 a year), for his father had been a truckman, and in his own youth he had chased Bill Redmond's trucks up and down the streets of the East Side. If he took this position, he would command a fleet of motor trucks such as were undreamed of in the days when his father had urged his horses through the welter of traffic on the cobblestoned streets, and he, who once carried orders (at three dollars a week) to Redmond's truckmen, now would be the boss truckman of all New York. He thanked Upham and Getz for the offer but reserved decision on it. There would be other offers. He wanted to spread them out before him and think them over.

As other proposals came along, some of them carried an even greater salary, but he quickly rejected them. Had he already, heartened by talks with Foley and Murphy, mulled over his first angry impulse never to return to public life, and, with an eye to the future, reckoned that a connection with one of the several great banking firms that sought him might prove an embarrassment to him in some distant campaign? Perhaps. At any rate, having taken counsel with his friends as Upham and Getz pressed him for an answer, he decided in favor of the trucking firm.

Whatever place politics held in his long-range plan, he concerned himself now only with business. He had been engaged to pull the company out of a financial rut, and he accomplished this by first making a careful study of its structure and then almost completely reorganizing it. Nor was he content to spend all his time in the office, but by getting about, widening his acquaintance among businessmen and convincing them that if they had any hauling to be done, they could best be served by the United States Trucking Corporation, he became the firm's best salesman.

Other matters engaged his attention. Before going into retirement on March 4, President Woodrow Wilson appointed him a member of the National Board of Indian Commissioners, and he, whose knowledge of Indians consisted largely of what he remembered of them from the days of Buffalo Bill's Wild West Show, gave some of his time to the affairs of the vanishing Americans, with special reference to the reservations on which some of them were living. In April, Governor Miller named him a member of the Port of New York Authority, created that year by the states of New York and New Jersey. He also became a director of the Morris Plan, the National Surety Company, and Pattison and Brown, wholesale coal dealers.

So efficiently did he manage all his duties that he could spend nearly all his evenings and Sundays at home. And, to his great joy, he could revive an old custom, that of walking with his children across the Bridge every Sunday morning to visit his mother in Brooklyn.

"That walk is one of the earliest and happiest recollections of my life," his daughter Emily has said. "Rain or shine, after breakfast on Sunday, Father would lead the small parade of Smiths across the Bridge, and even as we grew older, we found the walk thrilling and Grandma always seemed as glad to see us as we were to see her."

Now, except during school vacations when the older children were home, there were only Arthur and Walter to accompany him.

Al and Mrs. Smith reverted quickly to the social life of the old neighborhood, renewing old acquaintances, strengthening old friendships, revisiting old scenes. And the neighbors found it good to see, once more, the Smith family in a front pew at St. James's, where the Reverend Vincent dePaul Mc-Gean now was pastor.

In January, Al attended a prize fight in Madison Square Garden. This, in the minds of his friends, was a notable occasion, because he never had attended one before. As governor, he had signed the bill making prize fighting, or boxing, legal in New York state, but he had done so only under what amounted to mild duress. The bill was introduced by Jimmy Walker, now a senator. Jimmy, a great sports fan, had introduced the Sunday baseball bill which, enacted into law, had had Al's blessing, along with his signature, for while he cared little or nothing about baseball, he was in favor of the people going to a ball game on a Sunday afternoon if they cared to.

On the subject of prize fighting, however, he had a definite prejudice. In his youth he had, in common with all other youths of the period, an admiration for John L. Sullivan and felt badly when Sullivan was defeated by James J. Corbett, but his feeling for Sullivan seems to have been an instance of hero worship entirely divorced from John L.'s profession. Oddly, for one reared in a rough-and-tumble neighborhood, where street scuffles were common, he had a distaste for fist fighting and looked coldly upon the pugilistic heroes that rose on the East Side. He thought that all who fought in the ring were hoodlums, that those who surrounded them were worse, and that those who paid to see them were simpletons.

So, when the boxing bill came before him for signing, he shook his head. Walker pleaded with him, but at first in vain.

"The decent people of this state do not want prize fighting," he said, and believed it.

Walker laid before him letters from nearly a hundred clergymen of all denominations testifying to their interest in boxing and their approval of the bill. Bewildered, he read them through, one after the other. Again he shook his head.

"There must be somebody against it," he said, turning each letter over, looking for a joker in it somewhere.

"Only a lot of crackpots," Jimmy said.

Maybe it was the word crackpot that got him. That was a favorite word of his, crackpot. That was his word for the reformers or those who besieged him with pleas for weird laws of all kinds or who unreasonably criticized some law he favored. Or maybe the break came when Jimmy said, archly:

"I know you don't like boxing, Al. But you've always been a believer in the majority rule, and I am convinced, by the action of the legislature and the letters I have received, not only these"—with a wave of his hand toward the ministerial testimony—"but from hundreds of other persons, that the majority of the people of this state want boxing. You wouldn't stand in their way, would you—just because you do not favor the sport?"

Whatever it was that got him, he reached for his pen.

No one who knew him, however, expected to see him at the ringside, but there he was, right in the front row at the Garden on the night of January 14, 1921, as Benny Leonard, the lightweight champion, put his title on the line for Richie Mitchell of Milwaukee. The reason for his presence was not a suddenly developed interest in the champion and his challenger, however: a percentage of the gate receipts was to be donated to a fund for rebuilding those areas in France devastated by war, and Anne Morgan, chairman of the fund committee, had persuaded him to attend as part of the window dressing for the show. As it happened, he saw a great fight, both men being on the floor in the first round and Leonard winning by a knockout in the sixth. When it was over, Walker, who sat near Al, leaned toward him, beaming.

"Well, how did you like that?" he asked.

Al made a wry face. Walker howled.

"I'm afraid we'll never make a fight fan of you!" he said. They never did.

Meanwhile, Al had taken up golf. He never would learn to play it well, but he enjoyed the companionship the game provided. Now and then he made serious attempts to acquire some measure of skill, taking lessons from Jim Barnes, the professional, and reading Barnes's book on shot making. This must have opened his eyes to his own status as a player, for shortly thereafter he had printed and sent to his friends a book titled "What I Know About Golf, by Alfred E. Smith." It was handsomely bound, and the frontispiece showed him at the top of his swing. Beyond that and the title page were: "Keep your head down. Keep your eye on the ball. Follow through." And about two hundred blank pages.

Having reached the point where he could laugh at himself as a player, he got more fun out of the game than those duffers who—never quite realizing that's all they are and all they ever will be—strain and grunt and pant and swear in their efforts to knock a few strokes off their score and, when they fail, are disconsolate. He played all the courses, easy or difficult, attempted shots that would appall a professional, and exulted when, as happened once in a rare while, he brought them off. He never played more than nine holes, even when he took part in a tournament, where he was supposed to play eighteen.

"I won't be any better on the second nine than I was on the first," he would explain.

So he would multiply his score for nine holes by two, subtract his handicap and retire to the locker room, where he would sit for a couple of hours swapping stories with friends while the more determined and conscientious players slugged it out under a hot sun or in the rain.

In June of 1921 the Reverend Vincent dePaul McGean, pastor of St. James's, got a new assistant. Father James Kilroe, who had served in that capacity for a number of years, had been assigned to a church in Clove, New York, and in his stead there came to James Street, direct from the seminary at Dunwoodie, Father Arthur Gerard Keane.

Father Keane was tall—six feet four inches—but very thin.

"We'll have to put some meat on you," Al Smith said, the first time he saw the new curate. "I'll tell you what you do, Father Kane—"

"The name is Keane, Governor," the young priest said, mildly.

Al paid no attention to him. Kane it was with him and always would be, even when, years later, Father Keane, who had been away from St. James's for some time, returned as pastor.

"I'll tell you what you do, Father Kane," he said. "You walk around the neighborhood here. You'll smell Irish cooking, Italian cooking, and Greek cooking, and you cross over Chatham Square and you'll smell Chinese cooking. That will give you an appetite and you'll eat a lot and get to be a big fat man. Haw!"

To speed Father Kilroe on his way, there was a farewell party in the church auditorium. Father McGean, who would have presided, was ill, and the task devolved upon Father Keane. Although naturally somewhat nervous in his new surroundings, with so many strange faces before him and the most distinguished member of the parish on the stage with him, he acquitted himself well until he reached the high point of the evening.

"And now," he said, "I wish to present the featured speaker of the evening. Ladies and gentlemen, the former Governor of the State of New York, the Honorable——the Honorable—the—"

He came to a stammering halt and started all over again.

"Ladies and gentlemen, the former Governor of the State of New York, the Honorable—honorable—"

Smith, seated just behind him, could stand it no longer.

"Al Smith!" he barked, and got to his feet as the crowd roared with laughter and the young priest, his face crimson, retired to his chair in confusion.

Smith became very fond of the new curate and had a great appreciation of the work he was doing. Father McGean's illness persisted and the burden was heavy on Father Keane, but he bore it well. After mass one Sunday morning, Al said to him:

"You're doing great work, Father Kane! I was up to the Cathedral yesterday and I spoke to your boss about you. Yes, sir, I said to Cardinal Hayes:

" 'You've got a great young man down there at St. James's in Father Kane. Keep your eye on him.' "

Father Keane thanked him—and secretly hoped the Cardinal would know whom the Governor was talking about.

On another Sunday, while Father Keane was at work in his study after the last mass, Al, in cutaway, striped trousers, and brown derby, came in.

"What's the matter with the heat in our house?" he demanded. "It's as cold as the dev— Well, anyway, the women are all complaining. They have so many goose pimples I'm looking for them to sprout pin feathers any minute."

"I'm sorry," Father Keane said, "but I have nothing to do with the heat."

"Don't give me that!" Al said. "I know that while Father McGean is sick, you're running the show around here."

"Honestly, Governor, I don't know anything about it," the young priest protested.

"Where is the furnace?"

"Under the school."

"How do you get to it?"

"Well, the shortest way is down a manhole in front of the building."

"O.K. Come on. I'll take a look at it."

While a crowd of curious children clustered about the open manhole, the former governor of the state descended the ladder. He was up again in a moment, brushing coal dust and grime from his arms and shoulders.

"It's a Gillis and Geoghan," he said. "I'll have a man around to fix it in the morning. Don't try to stop him."

As he started across the street he said:

"I'll pay the bill, too."

It was about that time that the Catholic Charities were being organized for the purpose of preventing a duplication of effort on the part of the several societies within the church that were devoted to the relief and care of the poor. An outstanding layman was needed to head the new organization, and of course it was most desired that the post be filled by Smith.

"But," someone said, "he already has so much to do. Besides his own work, there are so many demands made on him that I don't know whether or not he would—or could—take this on."

And someone else said:

"Maybe if Father Keane asked him he would do it. He is very fond of that young man, you know."

So to Father Keane fell the assignment.

"Sure, I'll do it," Al said. "Tell me what I have to do."

"I don't quite know, myself, Governor. But I'll report your acceptance of their chairmanship. They'll be very pleased. And then, I suppose, you will hear direct what the duties are."

"O.K."

Al went back to some papers he had brought home from his office to study.

The next morning young Al walked into the rectory, bearing a huge bundle of pamphlets and books setting forth the aims of the organization.

"These arrived just now," he said, smiling. "Pop wants to know if you will look through them and give him a digest of them tomorrow."

The morrow was Sunday. Early in the afternoon, Father Keane called on Smith with a written digest of the material.

"That's great," Al said. "Sit down while I look it over.... Here, have a cigar."

Father Keane, a nonsmoker, feared the cigar might make him ill, but not wishing to offend his host, took one, removed its band as gingerly as though he were handling a time bomb, and accepted a light from Smith. He sat there smoking cautiously as Smith read the report. In a few minutes his head began to spin gently and he put the cigar in an ash tray. Having read the report through, Al looked up.

"Fine! Fine!" he said. "Now, when do we make the first move?"

"They want you to make an address at a meeting to be held Tuesday night in the Church of the Epiphany to launch the drive."

"O.K. I'll be there."

Father Keane started for the door.

"Hey!" Al said. "You forgot your cigar."

"Well, I—"

"You're not going to leave that, are you? Why, those cigars cost a dollar apiece! What's the matter? Don't you want to be seen smoking a cigar in the street? You haven't got far to go. You can palm it, can't you?"

"Why—er—yes. I hadn't thought of that."

The young priest picked up the cigar, forcing himself to smile, and having palmed it, rushed out into the open air. Safe within his own house a few minutes later, he tossed the dead butt into a wastebasket.

Al had so thoroughly absorbed the digest Father Keane had given him that at the meeting at Epiphany he outlined the plans of the Charities clearly to his audience without recourse to a single note. Father Keane remembers that well— and also remembers a story Al told him while they were wait- ing for the meeting to get under way.

"Here's a good one," Al said. "You know, my son Arthur just entered St. Francis Xavier school. The principal heard he was there and wanted to get a look at him, so he went to his classroom and said to the brother:

" 'Where's young Smith?'

"The brother pointed Arthur out and the principal said:

" 'I'm going to ask you a question in civics: Who was the forty-fifth governor of New York?'

"Arthur says: 'I don't know.'

" 'What!' the principal says. 'Don't you know your own father?'

"And Arthur says: 'Sure, I know Pop. But I haven't got his number.'

"Haw! Haw! How do you like that?"

18: THE CALL IS SOUNDED AGAIN

$\mathbb{S}$O PASSED 1921, A HAPPY YEAR FOR AL, A YEAR in which, with the political responsibilities he so long had borne removed from his mind—or from the back of his neck, as he once expressed it—he felt freer than he had in years. Political ambition may have stirred within him now and then, but mostly it was dormant. Then came 1922, another gubernatorial year . . . and now the office of the president of the United States Trucking Corporation became the meeting place for Democratic leaders from all over the state, alarmed by a movement, headed by Mayor Hylan, to win the party's nomination for Hearst.

This was distasteful to Smith, for in the background there was an old feud between Hearst and Tom Foley. Moreover, hadn't Hearst attacked him on the issue of the price of milk in 1919? Seldom one to hold a grudge, he held one against the publisher and agreed to use all the influence at his command to help block Hearst's nomination.

"There is only one way to do that," they said.

"And that?"

"Announce that you will run for governor yourself."

This he was reluctant to do at first, but the growing strength of the Hearst movement and the appeals of the leaders wore him down to a point where he was beginning to be convinced that in spite of the financial sacrifices a return to public service would mean to him, he would be shirking a duty to the people of the state if he refused to declare himself as a candidate. His complete capitulation was brought about by a letter from Franklin Delano Roosevelt, in which the future President, writing from his home at Hyde Park on August 13, said:

Dear Al:

Over a month ago I wrote to the conference of Democrats in Syracuse, urging that the Democratic party of this state must put its best foot foremost in the selection of a candidate this year. It appeared to me then that the sentiment of the overwhelming majority of Democrats was for your nomination again for the office of Governor.

Today, a week before the filing of designating petitions for delegates to the state convention, I am of the same opinion. I have been in touch with men and women voters from almost every upstate county and there is no question that the rank and file of Democrats want you to run.

Many candidates for office are strong by virtue of promises of what they will some day do. You are strong by virtue of what you have done. People everywhere know that in 1920, while you lost by a narrow margin in the landslide, you received a million more votes in this state than the presidential ticket.

More than that, your support came not only from Democrats but literally hundreds of thousands of Republicans and independent men and women who knew that you had given to this state an honest, clean and economical government and had consistently opposed the privilege seekers and the reactionaries.

These voters are not satisfied with the present conduct of affairs by Republican leaders in Washington and Albany. To them will be added many more who are sorry now that they voted the Republican ticket in 1920. You represent the hope of what may be called "the average citizen."

Something must be done, and done now. In every county the topic of political conversation is: "Will Al Smith accept if he is nominated?" Already unauthorized agents are saying that you will not accept, and many are being deceived and beginning to lose interest as a result. It would surprise you to know what enthusiasm would spring up overnight if we knew you would accept the nomination.

Frankly, I don't want to see things go by default in this most hopeful year, and that is why I am writing to you before the primary petitions are filed. I am taking it upon myself to appeal to you in the name of countless citizens of upstate New York, Democrats, Republicans, Independents, men and women, to ask you to say now, not later, that if nominated for governor you will accept.

We realize that years of public service make it most desirable that you think now for a while of your family needs. I am in the same boat myself—yet this call to further service must come first. Some day your children will be even prouder of you for making this sacrifice than they are now.

You represent the type of citizen the voters of this state want to vote for for governor, and you can be elected. The decision must be made now, as I have tried to point out. That is why, reluctantly to be sure, for I know what unselfishness it will call for on your part—I am asking you personally and publicly to accede to the wishes of so many of your fellow citizens.

Al wrote in reply:

Dear Frank:

I have your letter of August 13th and I have carefully read it. I appreciate your kindly sentiments, and they compel me to talk to you from my heart. I would not be entirely frank with you if I did not admit that evidence has been presented to me which would indicate a desire on the part of the Democratic rank and file that I again take the post of leadership. It has been and still is my desire to remain in business life for the reason you state in your letter—for my family's sake—but during the past twenty years I have been so honored by my party that even the members of my family would be dissatisfied if I did not answer the call.

Therefore, considering the facts as I know them, and answering your letter, I feel myself that I would be ungrateful if I were to say that I would be unwilling to assume the leadership. The state convention will be composed of elected representatives of the rank and file of the Democratic party throughout the state. They will undoubtedly come to the convention alive to the sentiment in their respective districts. If a majority of them desire me to accept the nomination for governor and lead the party in this state to what seems to me to be a certain victory, I am entirely willing to accept this honor from their hands and to battle for them with all the energy and vigor that I possess.

These letters sealed Smith's nomination and the doom of Hearst's aspirations to become governor. However, the publisher and his campaign managers did not immediately abandon their fight for political office but went to the convention at Syracuse determined to win the nomination for United States Senator. Hylan was in favor of this and even Murphy seemed amenable to it, but the Hearst forces either did not sense Smith's opposition to a place of any kind for the publisher on the ticket or underestimated the strength he could muster in a showdown.

The showdown, when it came, was one of the most dramatic episodes in Smith's political life. Some of the leaders, believing that without the support of the Hearst newspapers the success of the ticket would be placed in jeopardy, urged Smith to accept his enemy as a running mate. When he flatly refused to do so, tremendous pressure was brought to bear on him, even by some of his closest friends, in an effort to induce him to relent, but he shook them off almost savagely. Here was an indomitable fighter literally at bay, keeping to his room in the Onondaga Hotel and, while opening the door to his friends, closing his ears to their entreaties.

Murphy wisely kept away from him as lesser leaders retreated before his fury. Foley, proud of his resistance, kept away, too, save for one fleeting moment. Al was alone in the room, smoking one cigar after another, when the door opened and Foley's head appeared. He said but one word, but that was enough:

"Stick!"

And then he was gone. If Al needed any encouragement to hold out—although there was no sign that he did—he had received it from the man whose support he most valued, even beyond that of Murphy.

The Hearst forces were beaten and knew it. They were looking for a way out, and it came in a telegram from the publisher ordering them to withdraw his name from the convention.

The battle was over. From it Smith had emerged stronger than ever before. Although there had been no open clash with Murphy, he had not hesitated to risk it, and his flat declaration that he would accept the nomination only on his own terms had placed him forever beyond any form of domination, however slight, by Murphy or anyone else within the party.

His nomination was a mere formality. It was followed, as a sop to the Hearst-Hylan group in the interests of harmony, by the nomination of Dr. Royal S. Copeland, Health Commissioner of New York City, as United States Senator.

On Al's return to Oliver Street he was visited by a neighbor who wanted a favor.

"Al," he said, "I wish you would appoint my son to a job in one of the state departments. He is a very fine young man, as you know, sober, ambitious—"

A little surprised, Al said:

"But I haven't been elected. I've just received the nomination."

The visitor laughed.

"Why, you're in!" he said. "Miller hasn't got a chance to beat you!"

He was right. This time, with the immediate postwar hysteria dissolved, Al had his chance to present his own arguments to the people and to riddle those of his opponent. The outcome exceeded even the fondest hopes of the Democratic party when Al was elected by a record plurality of 387,000.

A day or so later Al had a visitor at his office.

"There is a Mr. Whitehead to see you," his secretary said.

"Harry Whitehead? Wonderful! Send him in!"

Harry came in, all smiles.

"Congratulations, Governor," he said. "You know, you're going to have an awful lot of people coming to you asking for jobs and I thought I'd better get my application in early. I'd like to go back to the mansion with you—if it's all right with you and Mrs. Smith and the children."

"I don't have to ask the rest of the family," Al said. "I know they feel as I do—that the mansion wouldn't suit us without you. I'll send word up right away that you'll be back with us—and we'll be looking for you when we arrive. I know you'll have everything in readiness for us."

"You bet I will," Harry said, happily. "Thanks, Governor. Thanks a lot."

There was another and more important figure returning to Albany. George Van Namee, who, at Smith's request, had resigned as his secretary to accept an appointment to the Public Service Commission in June of 1920, was quick to respond when Al asked him to take up once more his old duties at the Capitol.

19: THE SMITHS RECAPTURE THE MANSION

THE RECAPTURE—AND IT WAS NOTHING LESS than that—of the Executive Mansion by the Smith family took place on the thirtieth of December. Eager to get to work as soon as possible, so that he might fully carry out the platform on which he had campaigned, the Governor resigned his post at the head of the trucking company, took but the briefest holiday—scarcely longer than a long breath—following the election, and then plunged into the writing of his message to the legislature and the picking up of threads of detail dropped at his defeat two years before. Thus he was ready to move on Albany within five days after Christmas, which the family had celebrated in an apartment at the Biltmore.

No happier family ever set out on a journey. There was a crowd at the Grand Central to see them off, and the Police Department band was on the long platform to serenade them as they boarded the train. Endless bags, boxes, and bundles were carried aboard by grinning porters and stacked in the compartments. In addition to the luggage, there were a police dog, a Pekinese and a small monkey in a cage, the last a Christmas gift to the Governor from a policeman friend of his. The other passengers were almost—but not quite—as excited as the Smiths because of their presence on the train, and it was a gay trip all the way up the river.

Another crowd awaited them at the station in Albany—and another band. A wet snow was falling and the streets were ankle deep in slush, but while Mrs. Smith and the girls rode to the mansion in cars, Al and the boys marched up behind the blaring, thumping band, trailed by the cheering crowd.

On their arrival they found Governor Miller and
publican officials waiting to greet them.

The younger Smiths, having dutifully shaken
the retiring governor and the others, quickly made themselves at home, leaving their elders and rushing to the rooms
each had occupied before, which, to their delight, had been
arranged just as they were before by Harry Whitehead. And
Al, when the reception committee had departed, looked
about him, smiled at his wife, and said:

"It feels good to be home again, doesn't it, Katie?"

She nodded and began to unpack some of the bags they had
brought. Al wandered about, looking in this room and that,
sharing with the children their joy at being "home" again.
The chattering of the monkey in his cage attracted his attention.

"I think I'll let him out for a while," he said.

Mrs. Smith was dubious about the wisdom of that, but Al
said:

"Aw, he's been cooped up four hours."

He opened the door of the cage and the monk, finding
himself on the loose, made the most of his freedom. He ran
up and down stairs, perched above doorways, ran in and out
of closets, hung from chandeliers, and deftly eluded pursuit
by Al and the boys. The uproar ended only when Al, sub-
stituting strategy for exertion, sent one of the servants for a
banana. Lured by sight of the fruit, placed invitingly just
inside the door of his cage, the monkey stepped in and, immediately, was a prisoner again.

The monkey was the first occupant of a new private zoo
that Smith established on the mansion grounds. The fondness
of the returned governor for animals was well known, and
the presence of a monkey in the mansion led his admirers to
contribute to a collection that grew rapidly. This, at its peak,
included rabbits, deer, elk, pheasants, bears, alligators, terra-
pin, turtles, raccoons, foxes, owls, other monkeys, and a goat
called Heliotrope.

Now and then some of the inhabitants of the zoo created mild excitement by venturing beyond the grounds. A bear from the Adirondacks—he was very small when he arrived but by this time weighed over 300 pounds—got loose one day, climbed an electric-light pole outside the walls of a near-by orphanage, dropped over the wall, and joined a group of small girls at play. The children, not in the least afraid of the lumbering bruin, were delighted with him, but one of the nuns who conducted the orphanage suddenly appeared and, becoming frightened, telephoned to the mansion for help. Probably angered at the interruption of the game he was so greatly enjoying, the bear refused to accompany John Whitehead and the caretaker of the zoo when they arrived to take him back, and it was with some difficulty—and the aid of stout ropes—that he was returned to his quarters.

On another occasion four monkeys escaped. Al was at work at his desk in the Capitol when Walter called him on the telephone to give him the news of the simian break. As quickly as he could, he joined in the hunt for them and finally discovered them clustered in a tree on the grounds. This time the supposedly unfailing banana bait for monkeys at large failed to work. Instead, the monks, swinging from tree to tree, soon were out of sight, and the hunters, after a diligent search of the surrounding streets, had to admit defeat and go to bed. However, the next morning the four were discovered huddled in sleep in their cage, the door of which had been left open. Having explored the neighborhood, they obviously had decided there was no place like home.

Never was there a more informal atmosphere about an official residence than there was about the mansion during the second occupancy. This was even more pronounced than it had been through 1919 and 1920, for the children, being older, had a larger number of friends. The small boys who lived near by, or who were classmates of Walter's at Cathedral School, had the run of the house and grounds, for one of the first orders the governor gave was for the withdrawal of the

state troopers who so zealously had guarded the premises
during the Miller regime, and there was almost sure to be a
houseful of friends of the Governor, Mrs. Smith, and the
children.

Two or three nights in the week there would be a motion
picture show in the main hall, with the grownups in comfortable armchairs and Walter and his pals lining the broad
staircase behind them. An operator from one of the Albany
theaters, whom Al called the Professor, would rig the films
in a portable projection booth, and when the show was
about to start, he would stick his head out and Al would ask:

"Are you ready, Professor?"

"Yep," the Professor would say. And Al would bawl:
"Lights!"

Harry Whitehead would pull a switch, plunging the hall
into darkness, and the picture would be flashed on the screen.
All the newest pictures were available, of course, but Al's
favorites were any Charlie Chaplin picture—or any animal
picture. When the last reel had been shown and the screen
was dark again, Al would call out:

"Is that all you have for us this evening, Professor?"

"Yep," the Professor would say.

"Lights!"

And Harry Whitehead would pull the switch and light
would flood the hall.

Walter organized a baseball team, and appointed his father
as honorary president. This entitled Al to pay ten dollars a
year dues (no member of the team paid any dues, of course)
and to buy uniforms, shoes, bats, balls, gloves, masks, protec-
tors, and bases.

"We may not have been the best team in Albany but we
were the best dressed and the best equipped," Walter recalls.

Once in a while, although not often, the Governor would
lend his presence to a game played by the Capitol A. C. in a
park just a block or two from the mansion, but he wouldn't
remain very long. He didn't understand the game very well

and wasn't much interested in the little he did understand. But he took pride in Walter's athletic achievements, which surpassed those of the other boys, for Walter also played baseball, football, and basketball for Cathedral.

The fierce rivalry between Cathedral and the Christian Brothers school (young Al had attended Christian Brothers and Arthur was a student there now) was at its fiercest, perhaps, on the basketball court. It is doubtful if Al ever had seen a basketball game and it is certain he didn't know the first thing about it, but one night he agreed to toss up the ball for the first center tap when these two great rivals faced each other in a crowded gymnasium.

Not having the faintest notion of precisely what was expected of him as he took his place, the ball in his hand, the two centers in readiness to spring for it and the referee hovering about, he asked:

"Where do I throw it?"

"Just toss it up in the air," Walter said. "Wait till the referee blows his whistle and then toss the ball."

"O.K.," Al said. "Let's go."

The referee blew his whistle—and Al threw the ball up to the rafters.

Walter's athletic activities once landed him in the clutches of the law. He was playing stick ball—an early form of soft ball—in a street near the mansion and, being the catcher, was waiting for the pitcher to deliver the ball when, to his surprise, the other boys suddenly ran.

"Hey!" he yelled. "What's the idea?"

Just then he felt a heavy hand on his shoulder and whirled to find that the hand belonged to a glowering policeman. It seemed a neighbor had complained of the noise the boys were making and the cop, coming swiftly around the corner, had nailed the nearest culprit. Hauled off, unprotesting, to the station house, Walter was arraigned before the lieutenant.

"What's your name?" the lieutenant asked.

"Walter Smith."

"Where do you live?"

"One thirty-eight Eagle Street."

The lieutenant was writing it on the blotter.

"One thirty-eight—"

He stopped and looked up.

"Smith? One thirty-eight Eagle Street?"

"That's right," Walter said.

The lieutenant turned to the cop.

"It looks as though we've made a mistake," he said.

And then to the boy:

"I guess you can go back to your game."

Walter didn't say anything to his father about the episode at dinner that night, but the story was on the front page of the morning newspaper. Al chuckled as he read it at breakfast, but then he said:

"Let that be a lesson to you. After this, play on the grounds or in the park."

Just before Thanksgiving, a poultryman sent the Governor a handsome white turkey which, very much alive, arrived in a crate. On the tag attached to the crate was written:

"For your Thanksgiving dinner, Al. Hope you find him tender."

Al looked at the proud bird.

"He's too good-looking to eat," he said. "Put him in the zoo."

And so the turkey, which had been headed for the roasting pan, had its life spared.

The Governor, an early riser, had breakfast with the family every morning, but Sunday breakfast was the one to which they all looked forward, for then the family could linger longer at the table. They received communion at an early mass and then trooped back to ham or bacon and eggs, or sausages and wheat cakes or chops and hashed-in-cream potatoes, for the Smiths all had good appetites.

20: NIGHTS WHEN THE CONDEMNED SAT WAITING

PLEASANT DAYS AND NIGHTS IN THE MANSION and the Governor's fame widening...and nights that the Governor dreaded. These were execution nights at Sing Sing, when the condemned sat in their cells awaiting the coming of the keepers to lead them to the chair...and the Governor sat by an open telephone wire to the office of Warden Lewis E. Lawes at the prison, making certain that if a last-minute call should come for a reprieve, he would be there to receive it. There were no guests at the mansion on nights when a man...or a woman...was to die at Sing Sing, and the children always would remember their father, solemn and silent at the dinner table, and then going upstairs to his study and sitting, silent, by the telephone. Not until Lawes, at the other end of the wire, would tell him that the execution was over would he go to bed, his heart heavy.

Because of the length of time he spent in office, more persons were electrocuted in his administration than in that of any other governor of New York, yet he never became hardened to the taking of a life in that grim building within the walls of Sing Sing. Indeed, more than any other governor, he felt the weight of the responsibility that rested upon him when, with a word or a nod or the scratch of a pen on paper, he could snatch a murderer from the death house. The pleas of the condemned's relatives, which he never refused to hear, tore at his heart, and he repeatedly urged that a board be appointed to give a final answer to these pleas. But his urgings were in vain.

He knew that his natural sympathy for anyone faced with

the chair must be put aside and that he must act in strict accord with the law in all cases where clemency was sought. If there was any doubt in his mind of the prisoner's guilt, no matter what the judgment of the Court of Appeals might be, he did not rest until that doubt had been cleared up, in one way or the other. Once satisfied that a reasonable doubt remained, he would commute the sentence. In one case ... that of a friendless man for whom no one had spoken after his sentence had been affirmed ... he was sure that the manner in which the evidence had been presented, rather than the evidence itself, had brought about the verdict of guilty. Having commuted the sentence to life imprisonment, he worked tirelessly until he brought about a new trial, in which the man was convicted of second degree murder.

They tell a story in Oliver Street of a midnight visit by the Governor to a death-house cell that held a young man whom the Governor had known as a boy.

"I can't sleep, thinking of you," the Governor said. "I am convinced, in the light of the evidence, that you are guilty ... but tell me the truth: did you kill that man?"

The prisoner put out his hand.

"Thanks for what you did, Al," he said. "I killed him, all right. Now, go back to Albany ... and go to sleep."

Where there was no doubt in his mind, nothing could sway him and nothing prevent that fateful march which has been called the last mile. Sympathy for the condemned ... for an aging mother on her knees before him at a hearing ... for a tearful young wife ... or for children taken to plead with him, knowing only that their father must die if this man would not save him ... these affected him deeply, but he would not permit them to swerve him from his duty.

Those who sought to trade on an old friendship to save the life of a killer drew only a rebuke from him. There was a man who had been close to him for years and, much to his surprise, appeared at the Capitol one day to beg for the life of a hardened criminal who had been convicted of the fatal shooting of a bartender in the course of a saloon stickup. The Governor, who was not even aware that his friend knew the hoodlum, listened to his plea in amazement, until the friend reached the point where he said:

"You know, Al, I have never asked many favors of you, but as an old friend I want you to do this for me. . . ."

The Governor said:

"You ought to be ashamed of yourself to come to me on a mission of this sort."

On another occasion, a lawyer who had arranged for a final hearing for his client was callous enough to put in the time between New York and Albany drinking bootleg liquor in a friend's drawing room on the train. So far as his appearance was concerned, he was sober enough when he began to address the Governor, but his tongue quickly betrayed him.

"You're drunk," the Governor said coldly.

Turning to the wife of the convict, he said:

"I'd advise you either to get a new lawyer or sober this one up. I'll postpone the hearing for a day in order to give your husband every break I can."

The lawyer, sober and penitent, was back the next day, but it was no use. He couldn't talk his man out of the death house.

The plight of those awaiting execution was on his mind no matter where he was. One night he and George Van Namee, having come down from Albany in the afternoon, went to a show in a theater on Forty-fourth Street and Van Namee noticed he seemed restless and preoccupied during the first act. When the act was over, he said:

"Come on. Let's take a walk."

Van Namee thought he simply had been bored by the show and had seen all he cared to, but when they reached the sidewalk, he asked:

"You remember that stickup in this neighborhood for which that fellow is in the death house?"

Van Namee nodded. A man had walked into a poolroom

on the second floor of a building on Sixth Avenue between Forty-third and Forty-fourth Street and stuck it up. The proprietor had shown signs of resisting and had been shot and killed. Policemen, attracted by the shots and the uproar that followed as the gunman fled, caught a man in an alley leading from the rear of the building to Forty-fourth Street. In spite of his identification as the killer by other victims of the holdup, he vigorously protested his innocence, and among the questions raised at his trial was one that had to do with the time that elapsed between the firing of the shots and his capture. His story was that he had just walked into the alley from the street, seeking entrance to another house in the block, and, alarmed by the shots, had hastened out, only to fall into the clutches of a policeman running across the street. He could not, he contended, possibly have fired the shots and reached the mouth of the alley at the moment the policeman arrived.

His testimony was not accepted by the jury and he was convicted and sentenced to be electrocuted. His appeal having been denied, he had sought and obtained a hearing before the Governor, who had rejected his plea, and the date of the execution had been reset for the following week. Yet the case still weighed heavily on Al's mind.

"It occurred to me, as we took our seats in the theater, that we were just around the corner from the scene of the crime," he said to Van Namee. "I want to take a look and see if he could have reached the end of the alley as quickly as the cops say he did."

They walked around into Sixth Avenue and located the house. The door opening on the steep flight of stairs leading to the poolroom was unlocked, and Al pushed it open. There was no light on the stairs, and, looking up, they saw there was no light above.

"Come on," Al said.

They climbed the stairs, felt their way cautiously into the big room at the top, and, by means of a faint glow from the

street, found the light switch. The premises apparently had
been abandoned on the death of the poolroom proprietor,
for it was dust-covered and there was no sign anyone had
been there for a long time. A door in the rear led to a back
stairs descending into the alley. They opened it and peered
down. A light burned dimly at the end of the alley, faintly
illuminating its length. There were no twists or turns in it.

"He could have made it in no time," Al said.

He closed the door, walked over to the wall and turned off
the lights. "Let's go back to the show, George," he said.
"The second act should be just about starting."

21: BELLE MOSKOWITZ AND BOB MOSES

WHEN SMITH WAS DEFEATED BY MILLER AND subsequently appointed by him to the Port of New York Authority, he in turn appointed Mrs. Moskowitz to that body, and, as he had done in Albany, he frequently sought her advice on matters that came before him. Now in Albany once more, he continued to rely on her. He listened to her suggestions thoughtfully, and more often than not acted favorably upon them. If he did not always accept unquestioningly her judgment of men and affairs, he almost invariably was guided by it, and his faith in her was boundless. She was intrusted by him with digesting the sometimes lengthy data on legislative measures, and the concise reports she presented to him gave him at once a clear picture of them and facilitated his questioning of those who appeared before him at hearings on them.

As is inevitable in the case of any person so close to one in authority, Mrs. Moskowitz' scope of influence often was exaggerated, and it was said by the unknowing and the unthinking that she was "the power" behind Smith, dictating his policies, formulating his strategies, denying his aid to some and granting it to others without so much as consulting him, telling him what to say to interviewers, and, when it was necessary for him to make a speech, writing it for him. Ridiculous as this was, a belief that it was so was rather widespread, a circumstance that amused Al but was the cause of considerable resentment on the part of some of his friends.

On the subject of his speeches, one of his friends who had grown up with him in the Fourth Ward snorted:

"Anybody who knows Al Smith knows that isn't so. I don't say that maybe Mrs. Moskowitz doesn't advise him on some points or that she doesn't read over his speeches and, maybe, correct the grammar or put in a comma here and there. But anyone who listens to those speeches or reads them knows that it is Al Smith speaking because there is no other soul in the world who speaks like him."

That was true. And it also was true that many of his speeches, including those best remembered and most oft quoted, were not written at all but were delivered only with the aid of notes scratched on a sheet of stationery or the back of an envelope or any scrap of paper that was handy.

Naturally aware of the tales being told about her, Mrs. Moskowitz became extremely sensitive to them. She shunned publicity, and the political writers in Albany and New York, in respect to her wishes, refrained from mentioning her name except when it was absolutely necessary, knowing that it would embarrass her to see it coupled with Smith's in print.

But Mrs. Moskowitz was in Albany with Smith, and in New York, giving her thoughts, energy, and time to the furtherance of his career, devoting herself to a man who was so devoted to the people. She had found him a sturdy champion of the causes for which, as a social worker, she had fought so stubbornly and so long, and no task that might help him to achieve his purposes was too great—or too small—for her to undertake. She was willful and she could be arrogant at times in her dealings with those who opposed him, but to his friends she was thoughtful and charming. A frequent overnight or week-end guest at the mansion, she was especially popular with the Smith youngsters and their friends.

"She was a wonderful person to talk to," they have said. "She had the happy faculty of making us think she was just as much interested as we were in all the things in our lives— our school, our friends, our sports, and our hobbies."

Her own friends sometimes wondered why she, whose

capabilities were such that she could have commanded a large salary in private enterprise, should be content to remain in the service of the Governor and to draw but a minor wage. Friends they were, undoubtedly, but they failed completely to understand her when, to understand, they had only to look at the record of her life. Some of them urged her to seek office herself, but to these urgings she was coldly adamant. She believed that her place was where she was and she had no intention of abandoning it.

She must have known, too, that she could have been elected to almost any office she sought—if only because there were a number of powerful Tammany leaders who would have guaranteed her election to any post that would have removed her from such close contact with the Governor. Never quite certain just how much influence she had over him, they, who had none whatever, were jealous of her.

As to the exact extent of her influence, there were only two who could be certain—the Governor and Mrs. Moskowitz. Obviously she exerted a tremendous force in the workings of the Reconstruction Commission which, as Al repeatedly said, was her brain child and was made up very largely of persons of her choosing. Here, surely Al never seriously challenged her judgment, for she not only knew exactly what he expected of the commission but, because of her background and training, knew precisely the men and women who could produce the results he wanted. Thus she was responsible for his meeting with persons whose ideas coincided with his own, or, where he already was acquainted with them, with forging a closer relationship between them.

Robert Moses, most valuable of these allies, was one of Mrs. Moskowitz's recruits. Asked once how he became acquainted with Smith, he said:

"Through Mrs. Moskowitz."

"And how well did you know her?"

"I hardly knew her at all. But she knew of some of the

things I had done and asked me to work with the Governor. So, naturally, I did."

Moses was a frequent companion of Smith's in the two-year interval between the retreat from Albany and the return. Although Moses was a member of the Reconstruction Commission and, of course, of the New York Association as well, purely personal contact between the men had been slight through 1919 and 1920. With Smith in New York, a friendship had sprung up between them and they spent much time together at luncheon or dinner, in Smith's office or in late afternoon walks from the office to Oliver Street.

Although a Republican, Moses looked with jaundiced eye on Nathan Miller and devoutly hoped that Smith, in spite of his professed reluctance to seek the governorship again, soon would be re-elected to that office, to continue the social welfare campaign he had waged against terrific odds. For Moses was passionately devoted to the plans that either had originated with Smith or been so forcefully sponsored by him, and he was eager to ally himself closely with this man he so greatly admired.

A common aim had drawn together two men who had nothing else in common, judged against a background of the circumstances in which each had been bred, reared, and trained. Smith was a child of the poor. Moses was born to affluence. Smith was an indifferent scholar in the few years of his formal education. Moses had won scholastic honors in great universities here and abroad. Smith was a product of a rough and tumble political machine. Moses, with little practical political experience—although he was well equipped with sound political principles—looked with disdain on most of the politicians he had met. Yet these two were to join forces against those who opposed the ideas for which they stood, and the friendship welded in the battle would end only with Smith's death.

Moses was born in 1889 in New Haven, Connecticut, where his father had prospered as the owner of a department store.

When he was ten years old, the family moved to New York, and his preparatory education was gained at the Mohegan Lake School, near Peekskill. As a student at Yale he distinguished himself not only in the classrooms but as a member of the varsity swimming team, won a Phi Beta Kappa key, and was graduated in 1909.

From Yale he went to Oxford, where he excelled in jurisprudence, studied the British civil service system, and captained the swimming and water polo teams. On his return to this country he entered Columbia University, where he wrote a highly critical thesis on the British civil service for his Ph.D. He then went to work for the Bureau of Municipal Research, which was supported in part by the Rockefeller Foundation, and absorbed a knowledge of city and state affairs that brought him to the attention of Charles Evans Hughes and others, including Mrs. Moskowitz, who were interested in modernizing the obsolete constitution under which state departments operated. This had led eventually to his appointment to a place on the Reconstruction Commission.

Soon after he had met Smith for the first time, he was asked what impression the Governor had made on him.

"Oh, I don't know," he said. "I had heard so much about him from people who had been close to him for a long time that I was prepared to find him—well, just about as he is."

Later he was to say:

"He was an amazing individual. No other person I have ever known was even remotely like him."

Part of the reconstruction plan for which Smith now was prepared to fight with better weapons than had been at disposal in 1920 covered a hodgepodge of state parks and their administration. It was of great importance that new parks be created—and new parkways constructed to facilitate the rapidly growing automobile traffic throughout the state—but the first step in such a program must be unified planning and control. The fashioning of this new setup was delegated by Smith to Moses.

The situation into which Moses now plunged presented almost incredible difficulties. The haphazard growth of the state parks—even such as they were—had brought into being literally scores of administrative bodies working independently of each other, some reporting direct to the governor, some to various departments, and some, although supported by public funds, being under no control whatever. Moses first scrapped all these bodies—on paper—and many of their projects along with them, and mapped out his own plans to build broad parkways where rutted roads now twisted and turned, and to convert wild woodlands and barren stretches of sand into parks.

When his plans first were laid before Smith, the Governor snorted.

"Why, you're trying to sell the state a fur coat when all it needs is a suit of red flannel underwear!"

He had been keenly aware of the need for a development of the state parks, but he had not thought along lines as broad as those that Moses had sketched. Sure, the people needed more room in which to enjoy themselves but this was—why this was—

"This," Moses said, "is exactly what the state needs—and needs badly at present. At that, it is only a beginning. It will be expanded as rapidly as the demands for space increase."

Smith was dubious, but not for long. Good at arguing himself, he was good at listening, too. Within a short time Moses had persuaded him that his plans were sound, and from that moment on he was as definitely committed to the several projects as Moses was himself, and he fought for them as fiercely.

"Without his loyalty to me," Moses has said, "I could have done nothing."

No sooner was the program made public than attacks were centered on Moses from all directions at once. The little men who controlled the little parks denounced him savagely, threw every conceivable obstacle in his way, and sought by every means to bring about his removal. Contemptuous of them, he plunged on, confident that whenever he needed support, Smith would give it to him in the fullest measure.

One of those who bitterly opposed him was a wealthy New Yorker of Prussian descent—and Prussian arrogance. One day he stormed into the Governor's office and asked angrily:

"Do you want to settle this park fight?"

"Yes," the Governor said.

"Then I'll tell you how to do it."

"How?"

The visitor banged his fist on the Governor's desk.

"Get rid of Moses!" he shouted.

The Governor leaped to his feet, his face suddenly purple with rage.

"Get out of my office, you idiot!" he roared.

The visitor, shaken to his heels by the explosion, fled in terror.

Outraged, insulted, rendered more stupid than usual by his humilation, he went about telling everyone he knew about it.

"He called me an idiot! Me! An idiot! Why that—that—Bowery bum! To call me an idiot!"

Soon it was all over Albany. When Moses heard it, he laughed.

"Everybody knew he was an idiot," he said, "but the Governor put the tag on him."

The proposed Northern State Parkway, Heckscher State Park, and the Montauk parks precipitated a pitched battle in which no words reflecting on Moses were spared and nothing was left undone that was calculated to hamper him and, in the end, defeat him. He had commited the crime of invading, in the interest of the people, the sacrosanct precincts of the snobbish and reactionary rich and, too shortsighted to realize that what he intended to do would be of benefit to them also, they yelled to high heaven.

"That parkway will bring the rabble out here!" one of them screamed in agony.

The bleat went right over Moses' head, but it stuck Smith squarely.

"The rabble!" he bellowed. "I am the rabble!"

The legislature, preponderantly Republican, responded quickly to the pressure brought to bear on it by the frightened Long Islanders and smashed at the program, withholding appropriations for it and then offering to make them only under conditions that would have made it impossible for Moses to carry out the work. Smith called a special session in an attempt to impress the wisdom of the program on his opponents. He was beaten at that session, but the resourceful Moses talked so eloquently to some of his Republican friends who, he knew, were in favor of the program, that they succeeded in arranging a compromise under which the construction was begun. Once completed, it won the favor of even those who had been opposed to it at first, and its bitterest enemies were strangely reticent when the subject of their opposition was brought up.

Jones Beach, in the blueprint stage, brought on another terrific struggle, first with the Long Island towns which were asked, by popular vote, to deed the necessary property to the state, and then with the upstate legislators, who scoffed at the idea of beautifying a sandy waste and then expecting people to go all the way out from the city to enjoy the result. Little by little, however, Smith and Moses squeezed out appropriations, and when they had sufficient funds to build the foundations, work was begun.

The situation, trying as it was, was not without its humorous aspects. When the foundations had been completed, Smith and Moses took the chairmen of the Senate Finance and Assembly Ways and Means Committees out to inspect the progress that had been made. Unfortunately, when they arrived, they discovered that a storm the night before had completely covered the foundations with sand. The chairmen blinked in bewilderment, for they had been asked to go all that way to inspect something, and as far as they could see there was nothing for them to inspect. Moses was chagrined but Smith was only amused.

"It looks," he said to Moses, "as if that storm buried our hopes of getting any more dough, too."

But the sand was swept away and the money kept coming in, slowly, but, Smith saw to it, steadily, and in time this beach, unexcelled anywhere in the world, was finished. Not only has it been a source of pleasure to millions but it stands as a monument to the tenacity of Smith and his Park Commissioner.

22: THE NEWSPAPERMEN'S FAVORITE
GOVERNOR

AMONG THOSE WHO WERE DELIGHTED AT
Smith's return to Albany were the newspapermen
covering the capital. The veterans among them had known
him well through his years in the Assembly, and veterans and
Johnny-Come-Latelys alike had hugely enjoyed their association with him during his first term as governor. Miller
had been a far from satisfactory substitute for him, so far
as their personal relations with him had been concerned.
They admired Miller, but few of them could warm up to
him, for as they saw him, he was not the relaxed, even faintly
jovial man that he was among his friends, and he turned on
them none of the charm that had won the Smith children
when they had been prepared to dislike him.

Smith, on the other hand, was as he always had been and
always would be in any company. He was completely himself
at all times. The reporters, who had been allowed to see
Miller only at stated times, once more virtually had the run
of the governor's office with Smith again in the governor's
chair. He cracked jokes with them, with rare exceptions
answered their questions freely and frankly, and talked un-
restainedly with them, confident that none of them would
betray his confidence once it was understood that he was
talking off the record. Nor was he accessible to them only
when he was in his office. They were his companions on walks,
they wandered through the zoo with him, and they knew
that if they wanted any information from him at any hour
of the day or night, they could reach him on the telephone
at the Capitol or the mansion.

All of them were his friends, but none of the others was as highly regarded by him as was Charles S. Hand, of the New York *World*, already one of his closest advisers and later to serve him as publicity man.

There was in Albany at the time—in fact, he had been there for years—a professional reformer, who made an excellent living from the gullible by consistently attacking horse racing, prize fighting, Sunday baseball, card playing, and liquor. He had his regular contributors carefully indexed as to the amount they could be depended upon to give—anywhere from a quarter to a thousand dollars—whenever he tapped them, and if he didn't pray every night for a continuance of the evils he was attacking, he was exceedingly ungrateful. Smith, being a warmhearted, fun-loving, and intensely human person, was a regular target for his tirades, which amused rather than annoyed Al.

One day Al and Hand were walking down the hill from the Capitol when they saw the reformer approaching.

"Here comes that old faker," Al said. "I'll have some fun with him."

"How do you do, Doctor?" he said, cordially, as they met.

The Doctor, taken by surprise, was not a little embarrassed by his greeting.

"Oh! How do you do, Governor?"

"Is everything all right?" Al asked.

"Oh, yes, thank you."

"And how are the collections coming along?"

The Doctor shifted uneasily.

"Why—er—very nicely, thanks."

Al patted his arm.

"That's fine!" he said, heartily. "Any time you can make a lot of money attacking me, I'm for it. I hope you make a million."

He and Hand walked away, leaving the Doctor in a daze.

There was another, more serious occasion that Hand recalls, which gave the true measure of the Governor. Hand walked into the office one day at a time when he knew he would find Smith alone.

"Governor," he said, "I want you to do something—something important—for a friend of mine."

It wasn't Charlie's practice to ask for favors. Al was interested.

"Yes," he said. "Go ahead."

"This is a very fine man," Hand said. "Married, two growing sons, a good job and a nice home. The sons have become very much interested in political matters and they have been asking him how he voted on this question or that and how he intends to vote on issues coming up. What he can't tell them is that he has no vote. Years ago, before he was married, he was working in a bank, and, desperate for money needed at home, he stole six thousand dollars, was caught, and served three years in Sing Sing. For twenty-five years he has led a blameless life, has done well in business, and is adored by his family.

"I went to bat for him with Governor Miller last year, asking for a pardon and the restoration of his civil rights, but Miller turned me down. He said:

" 'I have made it a rule not to issue a pardon in a case like this unless three persons who have known a convicted person since he came out of prison furnish me with affidavits that he has led an upright life.'

" 'Why, he can't get three affidavits,' I said. 'His wife knows that he was in prison, but none of the friends he has today knows it except myself, and I didn't know it until he came to me the other day. You don't want the man to go around digging up his past life, do you, when it's a cinch that if he does, his boys will hear about it?'

"He just shook his head and said, 'I'm sorry. Unless I get those three affidavits—when I will take the matter under advisement—I can do nothing for him.' "

Smith started to say something to Hand but didn't. Instead, he called the executive pardons clerk.

"Mr. Hand will repeat to you the details of a case he has just given me," he said. "Make out the papers and bring them to me and I will sign them."

23: REPEAL OF THE MULLAN-GAGE ACT

OF THE MANY PROBLEMS SMITH HAD TO SOLVE in his political life, none was more difficult than that which was posed for him when in May of 1923 the legislature passed a bill repealing the Mullan-Gage Act. Of the many battles he waged on matters of principle with political foes—and friends—none was harder than that which he now had to wage with himself. This was another and very real crisis in his life, and there are many stories of how it was fabricated and how it was solved. There are some who believe that a sense of expediency got him into trouble in the first place, and that pressure and pressure alone got him out of it. There are others . . . and not all of them were overfriendly to him in his lifetime . . . who give him credit for having been guided throughout by only the highest motives, and having made his final decision not because of the pressure that undoubtedly was put upon him but because he had convinced himself that his earlier doubts were unfounded.

The Mullan-Gage Act had come into being during the term of Governor Miller. It called for state enforcement of the Volstead, or national Prohibition Law, and from the time of its creation it had been a source of heated argument and, in general, great dissatisfaction. It raised the question of double jeopardy and opened the way to widespread graft by state and municipal officers, and there is no question but that the voters who returned the Democratic party to power in the state in the 1922 election did so believing the act would speedily be repealed. This belief was justified when bills calling for repeal were passed by the Assembly and the

Senate and went to the Governor for his signature on May 2. Since Al frankly was opposed to Prohibition—he frequently had been the target of vicious attacks by the drys—it was assumed that he would sign the measure without delay.

It soon became apparent, however, that Smith was in no hurry to sign it. Day after day it lay on his desk. The Albany correspondents asked him repeatedly why he withheld his signature, and he either turned their questions aside with a joke or evaded them completely. A great uneasiness sprang up among the proponents of the measure. Newspapers favorable to it began to heckle the Governor. What had happened to him? What of the promises made by his party's speakers during the campaign that his election would mean the end of the Mullan-Gage Act?

Now reports got about that he was listening to advisers who told him that he had a great chance for the presidential nomination in 1924. That they warned him Prohibition was dynamite for any politician, especially one who, with presidential aspirations, must look to the South, where the drys were stronger. Reminded that Al never before had allowed his political ambitions to cloud his views on matters of principle, they shrugged. This, they said, was different. He was shooting now for the highest peak and he would let nothing stand in his way. What if he had opposed Prohibition before? If espousing its cause now would land him in the White House—well, many another man, looking to Washington, had changed his mind about a lot of things, hadn't he?

Meanwhile, letters, telegrams and personal appeals were piling in upon him. The wets urged him to sign the measure and the drys threatened him with political extinction if he did. He announced that he would hold a public hearing at Albany, in which he would listen to the arguments of both sides before reaching a decision. This quieted the uneasiness stirring within his party.

"He's simply playing it smart," the Democratic politicians said. "He's making a gesture to give the drys an idea they can talk him out of signing, but that's all it is, a gesture. He'll sign. Don't worry."

So none of them, including Foley and Murphy, worried any more—not until the Saturday night before the hearing, when, at a speech made in Brooklyn, he indicated that he would not sign the bill. Foley was startled when he read reports of the speech in the Sunday newspapers. He sent an aide to Smith to ask him if he meant what he had seemed to mean. The aide, returning, found that Murphy had joined Foley in an anxious conference.

"Well?" they asked.

The aide nodded.

"He says yes. He hasn't changed his mind about Prohibition but he has been studying this thing in its strictly legal aspects and he is convinced that repealing the law would do more harm than good. He showed me the clincher on the argument he has been having with himself. It was an opinion written by some judge in Brooklyn. And I guess he must have a very high regard for him. Anyway, in this opinion the judge sets forth his reasons why Al shouldn't sign the bill."

"Where is he now?" Murphy asked.

"He has gone back to Albany."

Late that afternoon a telephone call was put through to Albany by Murphy and Foley. They wanted to talk to the Governor and would, they said, be up in the morning. The Governor said he was just as eager to talk to them and would facilitate matters by returning to New York that night, which he did.

The meeting was held in Murphy's home. Since it originally was to have been held in Foley's home, his aide went to the Grand Central to meet Al and inform him of the change of plans. He accompanied Al to Murphy's house, but, invited to sit in and listen to the discussion, he refused. His subsequent explanation was that he feared there would be a row to which he did not want to be either a party or a witness.

"I'll wait out here," he said, taking a book from a shelf in the library and settling himself in a comfortable chair.

He waited almost all night. When the three emerged, Smith looked grim and the others plainly were worried. And when Smith had gone, the aide turned to Foley and asked:

"Well, what is he going to do?"

Foley and Murphy shook their heads and Foley said:

"We don't know."

The public hearing, held that week, drew a tremendous crowd.

"There were more white ribbons seen on Capitol Hill that day than you would see at a national convention of the W.C.T.U.," one reporter said.

The drys clamored shrilly for the life of the Mullan-Gage Act. The wets argued loudly for its death. The Governor listened patiently, intently, to every word that was said, although some that were said on either side were silly. In New York, Foley and Murphy kept in close touch with the proceedings. Fearful and hopeful by turns, they waited nervously for the decision. When it came, they drew a long breath of relief: the Governor would sign the repeal.

Accompanying the signing, Smith gave out a statement warning the people of the state of New York that the Volstead Law still was the law of the land and he would hold the peace officers of the state to account in their enforcement of it. Truthfully, no one paid very much attention to his words. The Mullan-Gage Act had been killed, and wets and drys alike knew that, in future, the federal enforcement agents would get very little help, if any, from the state officers.

From it all, Smith emerged as the outspoken political friend of the anti-Prohibitionists, and his political future, at least for the time being, was secure, whereas there is no doubt that if he had refused to sign the repealer, it would have ended right there, for New York Democracy would have disowned him. It was characteristic of him that, in reaching a decision so vital to him, he refused to take the easy way, and George Van Namee was to say of that crisis in his career:

"In all the time I spent with him, I never once heard him say, when a bill was placed before him for his signature:

" 'What will this mean for me?'

"The only question he ever asked when Jim Parsons, his legal adviser, and I had clarified some highly legalistic passages for him, was:

" 'Is this law good for the people of this state?'

"If it was, that was all he wanted to know. The bearing, if any, it might have on his future as governor or in any other position carried no weight with him.

" 'I am satisfied,' he once said to me, 'that as long as I do what I believe to be right, I won't have to worry. I am sure that any law that is good for the people is good for me, too.' "

24: THE NEW SUPERINTENDENT OF STATE POLICE

IN NOVEMBER OF 1923, COLONEL CHANDLER, the superintendent of the State Police, called at the Executive Office. The purpose of his visit was to tender his resignation.

"But why?" the astonished Governor asked.

His astonishment was understandable. The State Police, the very existence of which he had opposed in the beginning, had grown tremendously in favor with him, as it had with all the residents of the state. This was due in large measure to the care and skill that Colonel Chandler had exercised in his choice of officers and troopers and the sound plans he mapped out and followed. Because of him, the state troopers had become, from one end of the state to the other, symbols of courage and honor and efficiency. They had cleared out pockets of rural crime, solved murder mysteries that would have baffled village authorities, tracked criminals to the large cities and aided in their capture, made the highways and the lanes safe for travelers, and either prevented or put down disorders with which municipal police had been unable to cope. Called strikebreakers, at first, by labor agitators, they had acted wisely and discreetly whenever they were called upon to enter a struck shop or factory zone, favoring neither employers nor employees but being diligent only in the preservation of public order.

Now the man who was mainly responsible for all this was seated across the desk from the Governor telling him he had firmly resolved to retire. And to the Governor's question, "But why?" he answered:

"I have made up my mind to return to the practice of medicine, which I abandoned because I was so greatly impressed with the need of a state police force and felt that as a result of my studies of the matter, I was qualified to organize and direct such a force."

The Governor, loath to see Colonel Chandler's services lost to the state, tried arguing with him, but to no avail. As the Colonel had said, he had made up his mind.

"I still wish you would change your mind," Al said, "but since that seems too much to wish for, tell me, whom should I appoint as your successor?"

Colonel Chandler didn't hestitate.

"Captain John A. Warner, now commanding the troop at the White Plains barracks."

The Governor scribbled a note on his pad.

"Thank you, Colonel," he said.

It was the eve of Thanksgiving. On Thanksgiving Day, Captain Warner received a wire from the Governor:

"On the recommendation of Col. Chandler, I have appointed you Superintendent of the State Police. As of this date, your rank is that of Major. Please report to me in the Executive Office on December 1."

When the news of the appointment was made public, the newspapermen asked him about Captain Warner.

"What's he like, Governor?" they wanted to know.

"I haven't any idea," he said. "I never saw the man in my life."

That startled them.

"But—" one of them began.

"I know what you're going to say. That it's hard to understand why I should make an appointment of such importance as this without ever having seen the man. Right?"

"Yes."

"Well, I didn't have to see him. When Colonel Chandler insisted that I accept his resignation, I asked the man in whom I had the most confidence in that respect whom I should name to succeed him. The man, naturally, was Colonel Chandler. When he said at once that Captain Warner was his choice, I didn't have to go any further. Sight unseen, I'll bet my life on Captain Warner."

The Governor was wrong on only one point: he had seen Captain Warner. In fact, he had met him, and only a short time before. He, Mrs. Smith, Emily, and Catherine had attended a dinner given for Sophie Irene Loeb, noted newspaperwoman on the staff of the New York *Evening World*, at Briarcliff Lodge in October. Among the others present were Captain Warner, who was a friend of Miss Loeb's. He had been presented to the Governor, but as he was in dinner clothes, the Governor hadn't the faintest idea that he was an officer of the State Police and, if he caught his name at all, promptly forgot it.

There had been another occasion on which the Governor had seen him, but there was no reason for the Governor to remember that. During Smith's first term, he had presided at the dedication of a state institution in Westchester County, and that day his party had been picked up at the county line by a detail of troopers on motorcycles commanded by Captain Warner.

"The person I chiefly remember from that day, oddly enough," Warner has said, "was a young girl in the Governor's car who, somebody said, was his daughter. She had her hair in braids and a big blue bow stuck up on top of her head and she looked as though she were very pleased with herself."

In due time there was to be an argument on that point, the young girl, having grown up, denying that she wore her hair in braids at the time her father was Governor. She was, it developed, Emily Smith, whom the Captain met for the first time at Sophie Irene Loeb's dinner and whom he was to see more and more often now that he was going to Albany.

By background and training Warner was well equipped for the rank conferred upon him at Colonel Chandler's suggestion. A native of Rochester, he received his preliminary education at private schools and a public high school and then entered Harvard, from which he was graduated in the class of 1909. He was an officer in Squadron H, a cavalry unit of the New York National Guard, and was commissioned a captain in the State Police when that body was organized. His first command was at the Batavia barracks, where he put in one year before being assigned to White Plains. He had an excellent record as a police official and a leader of men. His main interest, aside from his work, was music, and he was well known in musical circles as a composer and pianist.

The Governor, who had no recollection of ever having met him, did not recognize him when, in obedience to orders, he reported on December 1.

"How do you do, Major?" The Governor said. And then, rather brusquely: "I don't know anything about you beyond the fact that Colonel Chandler says you are the man for the job. But I don't have to know any more than that. I want you to know this: I have the fullest confidence in you and will support you in anything you do. And if you ever want to talk to me, you can reach me without any trouble at any hour of the day or night."

"Thank you, Governor," the Major said.

And that was all—save that the State Police had a new and competent superintendent who was to serve in that capacity for twenty years, during which the force would be greatly expanded and reach new heights of efficiency.

25: DEATH OF MURPHY—AND A SET-BACK

EARLY IN 1924 THE DEMOCRATIC PARTY BEGAN to look within its ranks for a candidate who could defeat Calvin Coolidge, elevated to the presidency on the death of Warren Harding in 1933. William G. McAdoo, who was most prominently mentioned, had strong backing in the South and West, but other sections of the country were lukewarm toward him, and Murphy believed Smith had as good a chance as any to head off the former Secretary of the Treasury.

All his political life, Murphy had dreamed of seeing a man of his choosing go to the White House, and now he felt that dream was about to come true. He had entered Smith's name at San Francisco four years before to make the nation conscious of him, and in the interim Smith had grown greatly in stature. Some to whom he spoke of his plan shook their heads.

"You'll never make it," they said.

"Why not?"

"Smith is wet—and a Catholic. The country is dry—and Protestant."

Now it was Murphy's turn to shake his head. True, Smith was wet and the country dry, but surely there were issues other than Prohibition before the country. And, astute judge of politics though he was, he refused to believe that Al's religion would bar him from the nomination. Granted that a Catholic never had been run for the presidency by either party, he believed the religious intolerance he had known, even in New York, in his youth had been swept away by the years and that a man's faith would not shackle him if he were qualified for the office.

So he went ahead with his plans . . . but even as he looked forward with growing confidence to the battle, he was overtaken by death. Presumably in excellent health when he left Tammany Hall late in the afternoon of April 24, he suffered a fatal heart attack at his home the next morning.

No one was more deeply shocked than Al Smith. The close association between him and Murphy over a period of years had ripened into a firm friendship founded on mutual respect and admiration. It had been a long time since the Republican newspapers had referred to Smith as a mere tool of the Boss. They had been saying, indeed, that Smith now was the real leader of New York Democracy, that he had wrested control from Murphy that day at Syracuse in 1922 when he refused to run on the same ticket with Hearst. For once, anyhow, they were right. And yet Smith always had had a certain deference toward Murphy.

"Mr. Murphy," he always called him when speaking of him to others, and "Commissioner" when speaking to him.

"Mr. Murphy said so-and-so," he would say. Or: "I had lunch with Mr. Murphy today and I know he thinks . . ."

Whatever effect Murphy's continued presence on the scene might have had on Smith's future, his death brought to everyone a realization that Al now was, in fact if not in name, the leader not only of Tammany Hall but of the party throughout the state. Murphy's interest in him in the beginning had accelerated his rise from the lowest ranks of the party to the governorship. With Murphy's passing, his power, already great, had been increased.

In May, death was to strike even closer to him. His mother died at the home of her daughter in Brooklyn on the afternoon of Sunday, the eighteenth. She had, miraculously, come through two previous attacks of pneumonia, but they had weakened her greatly and a third attack was more than she could combat.

It is no tribute to a man to say that he loved his mother, but never had a man known a deeper love for his mother than Smith, nor been more devoted to her. She had taught him how to live and she was justly proud of him, yet his pride in her was even greater, if possible, than hers in him.

Now she was gone and he would miss her almost as much as he would have had she been taken from him in his boyhood, when she had made umbrellas and tended their little store and he had sold newspapers to keep their home together. There would be no more walks across the Bridge on Sunday mornings with the children to see her, no week ends in the mansion with her seated on one side of him and his wife on the other at the dinner table or, on winter nights, before the fireplace.

"It was the first real sorrow I ever suffered," he wrote.

It was a sorrow that swept from his mind all that had occupied it since Murphy's death—the reorganization of Tammany Hall, the plans for the national convention, which was to be held in New York in June, the countless decisions he had to make for those who had come to him for advice. A fearful blow had fallen upon him and it was necessary for him to go away for a short time that he might recover from it.

In June the delegates assembled in New York for the convention. It would not be as it had been in 1920, when Smith had been placed in the showcase at San Francisco and withdrawn as soon as the country got a good look at him. This was to be the real thing, the hardest and, up to that time, the most important battle ever scheduled for him.

Mrs. Moskowitz still counseled against his entering the lists. So did many of his other friends and advisers, deeming he had no chance to get the nomination and even less to win against Coolidge if, by some chance, he was successful in Madison Square Garden. But he shook off their advice. He was going ahead with a dead man's plans. Not liking McAdoo, and believing that McAdoo's nomination would not be a good thing for the party, he was confident that he could swing the majority of the delegates to his side. And after that? Well, the country was prosperous, settled, and smug, and Coolidge would be hard to beat. But Al never was one to chuck a fight just because the odds were against him, and he was of no mind to chuck this one.

Strangely for one who followed national political trends and movements so closely, he was not prepared for the strength and cunning of the Ku Klux Klan and its allies, the drys, as it advanced on New York, sworn to keep the nomination from him. When this was borne in upon him by the open hostility of delegates from the South, the Southwest, and some sections of the Middle West, he knew he was doomed to defeat. Franklin D. Roosevelt put his name in nomination, calling him "The Happy Warrior," quoting Wordsworth's lines:

> "This is the happy warrior; this is he
> "That every man in arms should wish to be."

But not even the rousing reception he received could delude him now. He was licked and he knew it, and sought only to block the nomination of McAdoo. This he helped to do, and the convention, long-winded, long drawn out, bitter, and in some of its aspects darkly ominous, resulted in the selection of a compromise candidate—John W. Davis, former solicitor general of the United States and ambassador to England.

Al promptly pledged himself to work to the utmost for the election of Davis and asked the candidate how he best could serve him.

"Run for governor again," Davis said.

This was not altogether to Smith's liking. Once more the urge to leave the arena and build an economic future for himself and his growing children was strong within him. The financial sacrifices he had made to return to Albany had caught up with him, and on the rebound from his defeat in the convention he could not work up a great deal of enthusiasm for another gubernatorial campaign. There was another consideration, equally important to him. He put it into words when, always the realist, he said to Davis:

"Suppose I carry the state and you don't?"

"Let's hope we both win," Davis said. "But what if you do and I don't?"

In Smith's mind was the thought of the direct threat to party harmony that had been bred by the convention.

"I wouldn't want to lay my supporters in this state open to suspicion of disloyalty to you because you received the nomination they thought should have gone to me."

Davis assured him that no one, least of all himself, would view the contingency he had outlined in that light and was insistent that Al run again as a duty to the people of New York state and the Democratic party throughout the country, since New York, as always, would be a vital sector in the election. And so, once more, Al answered the call sounded by his friends and at the state convention held in Syracuse in September accepted the nomination proffered by the delegates, who never had had anyone else in mind.

His campaign was a sham battle. For some reason not yet clear the Republicans had chosen as their candidate Theodore Roosevelt, Jr., an estimable young man but entirely without experience in the affairs of the state and absolutely inept politically. Al always had had a great admiration for his opponent's father, the late Teddy Roosevelt, hero of San Juan Hill and President of the United States, and was well liked by the entire Roosevelt family, whose guest he had been a number of times at Sagamore Hill. He would have preferred, in the circumstances, that almost anyone else had been pitted against him, but there was young Roosevelt on the hustings taking verbal pokes at him and he must put his personal feelings aside and not pull his punches.

Most of the punches he threw were counter punches. In his own speeches he made few references to Roosevelt but confined himself to the main issues before the state. But when

Roosevelt would hurl some criticism at him, he would repeat it and then say:

"I wonder who told him to say that?"

Constant repetition of the intimation that Roosevelt had no firsthand knowledge of the business of the state and was only parroting the words of Republican leaders had a telling effect on the voters, and Roosevelt was reeling badly when Al put the crusher on him. No one seems to remember what it was that young Teddy said, but that is unimportant, since everybody remembers Al's reply when he was asked to comment on it.

"If bunk was electricity," he said, "young Roosevelt would be a powerhouse."

No candidate ever before or since was so effectively disposed of in a single sentence. All that remained now was to count the votes. The result was as Smith had forecast in his talk with Davis: Coolidge carried the state by a plurality of more than 850,000 and swept most of the state candidates, as high as the Lieutenant-Governor, into office with him; but in the face of that overwhelming Republican victory Smith was elected with a plurality of 108,561.

26: THE THIRD TERM—AND INTO THE
FOURTH

ON JANUARY 1, 1925, SMITH WAS INAUGURATED
as governor for the third time. No better picture of
him could have been drawn as he stood in the crowded Assembly Chamber that day than was limned in the words of
his brief address. Here was a man honored, loved, eminently
successful, yet humble withal, speaking with deep sincerity
in one of the great moments of his life:

"History tells me that today I am the recipient at the hands
of the people of the State of New York of the signal and most
distinguished honor of being the first man in exactly one
hundred years to be inaugurated as Governor for a third
term.

"I approach the reception of this honor with a heart full
of gratitude. I am unable to make myself believe that there
is anything in any small accomplishment of mine in the past
to justify so great an honor.

"I come to my great office with no partisan mission. I feel
as if I were standing alone amidst the wreckage and disaster
that overtook the Democratic party on November fourth. All
that I can say is that I shall continue to give to the state
the best service of which I am capable.

"This is the sixteenth time that I have taken the oath of
allegiance to the state in this room. I have a deep and abiding
affection for the Assembly Chamber. It has been my high
school and my college; in fact, the very foundation of everything that I have attained was laid here. I approach this
term only with a desire to do what is best for the great State
of New York and keep her in the forefront of the common-

wealths of the Union, where she rightfully belongs. I have the desire and disposition, the heart and the courage, and thanks to God Almighty, the health to work hard, and I promise in this chamber and in His divine presence to give the people of the state the very best that is in me."

He had just marked his fifty-first birthday and he was in the very prime of his life. Both feet were firmly planted on a peak toward which he had climbed steadily since that day, twenty years before, when as a frightened fledgling assemblyman, he had entered that chamber for the first time. No man in the history of New York state ever had known the personal following and political power that were his. Almost alone he had survived the avalanche of Republican votes that had crashed upon his running mates, and he had survived because he had so many friends and supporters among the Republicans. He was governor of the state and leader of his party within the state. Disappointed though he had been by his rebuff in the national convention the previous June, he actually had gained strength throughout the country in that feverish week, for there were many leaders and delegates who, believing that he was not ready for the presidency in 1924, were convinced that he would be with the coming of another four years.

The plans which he had drawn up as long ago as his first term were bearing fruit now. Great public improvements for which he had fought so stubbornly either had been effected or were under way. State hospitals, asylums, and prisons that were overcrowded and antiquated had been or were being renovated and enlarged, and new buildings were being erected to bear the load. Parks, roads, bridges, and beaches were being fashioned as Bob Moses, his sleeves rolled up, worked untiringly. State departments were being torn apart and rebuilt, and the Albany air was thick with flying deadwood as Smith plied the ax. New departments, thoughtfully planned and properly staffed, were being created, and new state office buildings in New York and Albany soon would be ready for occupancy.

The radio, still in its infancy so far as its political uses were concerned, was seized upon by Al as a valued aid for getting directly before the people the projects on which he was working. He called it, at first, the "raddio," and although the proper pronunciation was brought to his attention, he continued to call it that because he knew that by doing so he delighted some listeners and, impishly, because it annoyed others. But, radio or raddio, his voice was heard over it frequently now, harsh but insistent, explaining the things he had in mind, deploring the obstacles placed in his path, attacking or ridiculing those who opposed him. And always his words were simple and his meaning clear, so that even when he was discussing complicated financial matters so foreign to most voters, no one ever could turn away from his set wondering what the Governor had been talking about.

Al may not have put baloney into America's lexicon of slang as a synonym for bunk, hogwash, or applesauce, but no one ever made more effective use of the word.

"Baloney!" he would thunder into the microphone, as his listeners chuckled or muttered angrily, depending upon their political leanings. And once when an opponent, objecting to that description of an opinion he had given, launched into a long and specious explanation, Al retorted:

"No matter how thin you slice it, it's still baloney!"

Eccentrics who threw their puny weight against his were dismissed as crackpots or—a word of his own coining—crackerloos. Those who challenged him on factual grounds, a hazardous and usually fatal thing to do, were invited to look at the record. Then, and in the four years of his active political life that followed, he would say:

"Mr. So-and-so declares that such and such is the case."

And, after a slight pause:

"Well, let's look at the record!"

The boy who had won medals for debating and strutted on the stage at St. James's had become the man who still loved nothing so much as a public debate and still, on a platform, was very much an actor. It was remarkable that after the first few demonstrations of his skill at debating before an audience he could induce anyone to oppose him in a public free-for-all. The fact remains that, one by one—and sometimes two by two—they were inveigled into tangling with him. Once up there, they realized that they were but amateurs combating a professional, and any humane prize-fight referee would have stopped the slaughter after the first round.

There were, as there always would be where he was in action, times out for laughs.

Elihu Root called on him one day to say that he would like to donate a bust of the late President Chester A. Arthur to be placed on exhibition in the Capitol. Smith replied that it was an excellent idea and thanked Root for his thoughtfulness, and Root departed, saying that he would immediately commission a sculptor to do the bust. At dinner in the mansion that night, Al told Bob Moses about it, and the next morning Moses, who was staying with him, said at the breakfast table:

"You know, I was thinking about that bust of Arthur last night, after we'd gone to bed."

"Yes?"

"And there's something that didn't occur to either of us when you mentioned it: you'll have to have the permission of the State Art Commission before you can accept it."

"Who says so?"

"I do. I ought to know. I'm a member of the commission."

Al buttered his toast.

"That's ridiculous," he said.

"So is the commission," Moses said, "even if I am a member of it. But that's your fault, not mine. You signed the bill creating it, and although I'll admit you must have nodded

when you did it, I should think"—with a wink to Mrs. Smith
—"the least you could do is to read a bill before signing it."

"I did read it!" Smith said, indignantly. "I never signed a
bill in my life before reading it thoroughly."

"Then I'll refresh your memory on this one," Bob said.
"The bill sets forth very clearly that no object of art may
be accepted by the state without the approval of the commission. If you doubt me, I'll get a copy of the law and
show—"

"Never mind. I'll take your word for it. Oh, well, they'll
approve it."

There was a meeting of the commission that day and, to
Bob's amusement, the Governor's application was denied.

"What are you grinning about?" the chairman asked.

"I can't tell you right now," Moses said, "but I have a
hunch you'll find out."

Word of the commission's action reached Smith during a
recess. Almost at once the chairman was advised that the
Governor wished to see all the members in his office as soon
as possible. Trailed by the still grinning Moses, they filed
apprehensively into the Governor's presence.

"Be seated, gentlemen," Al said.

He stood up, picked up a sheet of paper that lay on his
desk. From where they sat, the commissioners couldn't see
it, but it was blank.

"I have before me a resolution," he said. "I would like to
read it to you."

He cleared his throat.

"Inasmuch as Elihu Root, a distinguished statesman, has
offered to donate to the State of New York, for exhibition in
the Capitol at Albany, a bust of the late Chester A. Arthur,
President of the United States, and inasmuch as Mr. Arthur
was long a resident of this state and his career reflected great
credit upon it, as well as upon himself, and inasmuch as the
Governor of this state looks with favor on Mr. Root's gesture,
be it resolved . . ."

His chin was thrust out belligerently and his face had reddened angrily.

"Be it resolved that the State Art Commission is full of baloney!" he yelled.

He sat down.

"That's all, gentlemen," he said. "You may go."

They withdrew hastily. Visitors to the Capitol today may see a bust of Chester A. Arthur, donated to the state by Elihu Root.

No one ever gave as much time to the affairs of the state as Smith, nor more completely enjoyed doing so. He reveled in the battles he was called upon to fight, relaxed easily between them and concentrated on the routine matters that came before him, followed with interest every bit of legislation that was introduced, and always was accessible to callers at his office. These ranged from schoolchildren and honeymooning couples who just wanted to look at him and shake his hand to newspapermen, businessmen and politicians who had something to say to him and wanted from him, in return, stories, advice, or, in some cases, favors.

Once he had disposed of the business at hand, he delighted in sitting around with them, telling stories or listening to them, asking questions of his own, discussing small matters of interest to him and to them. On many a late afternoon he would say to George Van Namee:

"Well, George, looks as though we won't get much more done here today. Let's all go up to the house."

And he and Van Namee and the guests would get up and walk to the mansion, stopping, perhaps, to inspect the zoo. Mrs. Smith never knew how many to expect for dinner, but she and John Whitehead always were prepared for as many as Al brought with him. Once in the mansion—once, indeed, he had left his office in the Capitol—the business of the state was put away for the time. He was a man come home with his guests for dinner with his wife and children. Often, after dinner, there would be games in which the young Smiths would take part, or a movie, and if the guests who regularly were invited ever tired of the fare of comedies or animal pictures on the screen, none complained.

"I think Mrs. Smith and the girls would have liked a little romance in their pictures once in a while," Van Namee said, looking back on those days and nights, "but they knew Al never would sit through the love scenes."

But if there was no romance on the screen, it was abroad in the house, although the Governor seemed to be the last to recognize it. Alfred, Jr., had been married quietly, in 1924, and Arthur in 1925, but Al apparently had given no thought to the likelihood that his daughters soon would be following them into matrimony. He recalled, later, that as 1925 wore on, a frequent guest at the mansion dinner table was Major Warner, but he was pleasantly surprised when Emily informed him, late in the year, that she and the Major had become engaged. And now there was a smiling newcomer seen often about the mansion, especially when Catherine was having guests. His name was Francis Quillinan. He was a Cornell graduate, a lawyer and a son of the District Attorney of Rensselaer County.

Smith, liking him at once and discovering that he also played golf, had him out to play with him many times. One day as they were setting out, Al said to the driver of his car:

"Stop down at that sporting goods store where I get my stuff."

When they reached the store, he said to Quillinan:

"Come in with me."

Inside, he said to the clerk:

"Give this fellow a decent set of golf clubs, will you?"

Startled, Quillinan asked:

"What's the matter with my clubs?"

"Haw! Haw!" Smith roared. "I don't wonder you can't get around the course with those things! They give me the willies."

The clerk brought out a set of matched clubs.

"Swing a couple of those and see how you like them," Al said to Quillinan.

The young man plainly was delighted with them.

"All right," Al said. "Let's get started."

And to the clerk:

"Charge 'em to me. Maybe they'll make a golfer out of this young fellow."

Emily and Major Warner were married in Albany on June 6, 1926. They had a large wedding, which attracted many of Al's old friends from New York who had known Emily practically from the day she was born.

"Even Louis Fook was there," Al said.

Louis Fook was the Mayor of Chinatown.

Also in the party from New York were many of the city's political leaders, and when the reception was over and the young couple had departed on their honeymoon, the talk at the Governor's table turned to politics. A single theme ran through the talk: he must run for governor again or his party, weakened by the blow that had fallen upon it in the 1924 election, would invite new and even heavier blows.

"Let's talk about that some other time," he said.

So they remained in Albany for several days to talk about it. Smith had given another demonstration of his still growing political influence by the vital support he had thrown to Jimmy Walker in the fall of 1925, when Walker had triumphed over Hylan in the city's Democratic mayoralty primaries and then moved on to victory in November. Now that influence would be desperately needed once more if all were not to be lost in the state. They pointed out that the Republicans undoubtedly would nominate Congressman Ogden L. Mills, one of New York's foremost citizens, socially and financially, who surely could defeat any lesser candidate the Democrats might put forth. It was obvious, they said, that only he could fend off Mills.

He was not at first receptive to their arguments, contending that he certainly was not the only man within the state Democratic party would could win and that, after the years of service he had rendered to the state, he was entitled to retirement to private life. But when they asked him to name someone else who could win, he had to confess that he was at a loss to do so. No one went very deeply into his notion that he had earned a rest. When their pleas were bolstered by those from men and women throughout the state whose opinions he valued, many of them Republicans, he acceded.

The battle line was drawn as the leaders had believed: Smith against Ogden Mills. It was not a very exciting campaign. Mills, badly advised, sought to counter the issues Smith hurled at him with some of his own—and then discovered he had none to hurl back. Chiefly remembered from that campaign is a night at Tammany Hall when a maneuver Al had carefully rigged went awry, to his own amusement and the discomfiture of a friend.

The Hall had been chosen as the site for a speech that was to be built around a question Smith wanted injected so that he might put across a telling answer, not for his immediate audience but for the wider audience he would reach by newspaper and radio. This was explained by him to a friend by the name of Tom O'Brien who, a stranger to the regulars at the Hall, would be carefully planted about halfway back in the crowd to act as his stooge.

"I'll open with a few generalities and then go over some of the ground I've covered in previous speeches," Al said. "There will be about five minutes of that and then, when you see me fingering my tie, like this, you get up and say:

"'Governor, I'd like to ask a question.'

"I'll say: 'Very good, my friend. What do you want to know?'

"Then you spring this question on me—I'd been hoping Mills would ask it, but he hasn't, so we'll have to do it this way—and I'll start right from there and go into my real speech. O.K.?"

"Sure," Tom said. "Anything you say, Governor."

The Hall was packed, of course. When the uproar following his introduction had died down, Al began his talk. The crowd listened, eager, enthusiastic, frequently cheering. At the appointed time, he paused, fingered his necktie and seemed about to resume when, taking the cue, O'Brien stood up.

"Just a moment, Governor!" he said, loudly. "I'd like to ask you a question!"

Around him, men growled menacingly. From all over the hall, heads were turned in his direction. Someone yelled: "Throw the bum out!"

"No! No!" Al cried. "Let us hear what the man has to say!"

"We'll take care of him, Al!" a man shouted.

Those nearest the hapless O'Brien seized him, hauled him from his seat, hustled him down the nearest aisle and threw him into the street.

"All right, Al!" somebody said. "You can go on now."

Almost unable to control his mirth, he managed to proceed.

"I think I know what that man was going to ask me," he said. "I'll tell you what it was."

He did.

"And now, although he no longer is with us—"

The Hall rocked with laughter.

"Now, although he no longer is with us, I'll give him his answer—and he can read it in the newspapers tomorrow!"

The crowd howled.

As soon as he could get away from the Hall after the speech, Al sought out his rueful and slightly bruised friend O'Brien.

"I'm sorry, Tom," he said. "But you put me over, anyway."

O'Brien scowled.

"You know I'd do anything in the world for you, Al," he said, "but the next time you want me to stooge for you in Tammany Hall, you'll have to give me better lines."

The campaign rolled on smoothly. Everyone, including

Mill's advisers and publicity men, played directly into Smith's hands, and he won by a plurality of 257,000.

On January 1, 1927, he was inaugurated for his fourth term. On that occasion they hauled out and dusted off a historic chair for him. It was the chair upon which once had sat Governor George Clinton, the only other four-time winner in the history of the state.

27: FOLEY'S DEATH—AND FAREWELL TO OLIVER STREET

IN THE MEANTIME, TWO TIES HAD BEEN SEVered which had bound Smith to the old Fourth Ward. One was his abandonment of the house at 25 Oliver Street, and the other was the death of Tom Foley.

No one, perhaps not even himself, knew when he returned to Albany in 1923 that he never would go back to Oliver Street, but it was so, and if it was not in his mind then, it would be shortly. Experience had proved that the old house no longer could serve the needs of the family as it had in years gone by, and Al learned that if he did not renew the lease, St. James's Church would not be displeased, since there was some thought of converting the house into a convent for the nuns who now taught in the school. He and Mrs. Smith talked the matter over at length and decided that since they were to be in Albany for two years—they could not foresee, of course, that they would be there for six—it would be wise to let the house go. One of the considerations that prompted them to reach this decision was financial. His election to serve another term as governor had been gratifying to him, naturally, but it had cost him $40,000 a year, or the difference between the $50,000 he received from the United States Trucking Corporation and the $10,000 which at that time New York paid its chief executive. By giving up the Oliver Street house, he would be relieved of the burden of maintaining two homes at once, which was important, since the allowance he received for expenses at Albany did not begin to cover his expenses there.

Unfortunately—but almost inevitably—when it became known that the Smiths no longer would live on Oliver Street, resentment was felt by some of the neighbors.

"He's too big for Oliver Street," they said, disdainfully. "The old neighborhood isn't good enough for him any more. Stuck up, that's what he is."

Many of their other old friends or relatives had left the neighborhood and that was all right. But Smith was different. Smith had made Oliver Street famous. Hadn't he said, when first elected to the governorship: "My home in Oliver Street will remain my New York home no matter where my work shall take me, and when I come to the city at any time, there I shall live"?

Now, in 1924, he had put the old neighborhood behind him. When he came to New York, he lived at the Biltmore, no less. Well, there it was. They had been his friends and stuck with him all through the years and voted for him, no matter what office he sought. But now he had turned his back on them.

They overlooked the fact that he seldom came to New York that he didn't appear at the Downtown Tammany Club, just as he used to when he was an assemblyman, and they knew, although they were not ready to admit it, that their problems were as close to him as they had always been. Some of them never got over it, and to this day traces of that old resentment linger.

Foley died in 1925. Robust all his life, he refused to take to his bed when he contracted what he thought was no more than a heavy cold; but Smith, in Albany, was alarmed at reports of Tom's growing weakness. With Dr. Matthias Nicoll, Jr., the State Health Commissioner, he hurried to New York and went at once to Foley's home at 15 Oliver Street. A brief examination by Dr. Nicoll disclosed that Foley had pneumonia, and although he protested volubly that there was nothing wrong with him but a cold in the chest and a pain under his right shoulder, he was removed almost forcibly to a hospital, where he died a few days later.

Smith, who had gone back to Albany believing Tom would fight off his illness now that he was getting proper care, was informed at once of his death, and newspapermen who gathered in his office that morning found him greatly saddened.

"I knew Tom Foley as long as I can remember," he said. "I was born within a few blocks of his saloon. I used to go on the outings he had every summer . . . and I remember election nights around his club. Everybody in the neighborhood knew him and how good he was, and how charitable. . . . I don't know how much money he had when he died, but I'll bet he didn't have a nickel. He was a good businessman and he made plenty, but he gave it away.

"He was responsible for my first nomination . . . he and a man by the name of Henry Campbell, a grocery man on Vesey Street. When I came to Albany for the first time, he told me never to open my mouth unless I knew what I was talking about . . . and never to make a promise unless I knew I could keep it. . . . That's the way he always was. . . . I hope I've been like that."

He smiled a little.

"Another time he said to me:

" 'Always remember, Al, that to kid anybody else is a venial sin—but to kid yourself is a mortal sin.'

"He will be buried from St. James's Church. His wife was christened there—Tom, himself, didn't come to this country until he was twenty-two—and he and Mrs. Foley were married there. He was . . . a great man. He was my friend."

Forty years passed before him as he spoke. Forty years and more, for, as he said, he had known Tom Foley as long as he could remember. In the beginning, Foley had been the big ex-blacksmith, the saloonkeeper, the political boss upon whom he once had looked in awe, the benevolent despot of the district who had parties at Christmastime and picnics in the summer. As he grew older, he knew that this was the man

who could make or break anyone in the neighborhood ...
and that he made far more than he broke. He knew that this
was the man who paid the rent for those who were threatened with eviction and bought coal for those who were too
poor to buy it for themselves. That this was the man to whom
the people of the neighborhood turned when they were in
trouble of any sort, confident that he would see them through
it. The man who, when they died, would follow them to the
grave and, if they died destitute, pay for the grave itself.

Foley had been his political sponsor and tutor. Foley had
given him his first chance to go to Albany and had watched
his steady climb with a pride that he could see in Foley's
eyes. There had been differences between them, of course, as
they had come down the years together, as there were bound
to be between any two strong-minded men, but always those
differences had been resolved in quick, honest conversations.
He had outgrown Foley. The time long had passed when he
needed Foley's influence. But they never spoke of that. The
friendship between them was so close, so binding, that only
death could end it.

Foley had two houses in New York, one on Thirty-fourth
Street, the other at 15 Oliver. But the Oliver Street house he
called home, and there his body lay. There were gathered,
now, to see him on his way, men from the high places in the
life of the city ... and old neighbors ... and rogues and
scoundrels who, at some time in their lives, had been helped
by him: a sharp-eyed reporter picked out of the crowd that
moved endlessly in and out of the house a man who had just
completed a term in Sing Sing, and the judge who had sent
him there.

Through that sorrowing crowd walked the Governor, his
head bowed, his heart full of grief.

They tell a story of Al Smith and St. Peter's Church in
Pleasantville, New Jersey, which goes like this:
In the spring of 1926, Al went with some friends to the

Sea View Golf Club, near Absecon, on the New Jersey coast, for a week end of relaxation and play. They golfed on Saturday afternoon, and before settling down to a poker game after dinner they asked the manager of the club where they would find the nearest Catholic church in the morning, as they wished to attend an early mass. The manager thought for a moment—he could have directed them to any one of a number of churches in the vicinity—and then he said:

"Well, there is a little church in Pleasantville where some of our members go once in a while."

"Pleasantville, eh? O.K."

So they went to Pleasantville for seven o'clock mass, and when the collection plate was passed they threw ten and twenty and fifty-dollar bills on it. Now this was a very poor church and the pastor, Francis J. McCallion, seldom had seen a ten-dollar bill on the plate and never so much as a twenty, and he asked, puzzled:

"Where did all this money come from?"

"Governor Smith of New York and some of his friends were here," he was told.

"Governor Smith!" he exclaimed. "What is he doing here?"

On learning that Al was at the Sea View Club, he went there immediately and found the Governor at breakfast.

"I felt that I must come over and thank you in person, Governor," he said. "You have no idea how much your generosity and that of your friends means to our church."

And out of that meeting and the tale the young priest told of his struggles with a poverty-ridden parish grew the determination of Smith and his friends to aid him with their contributions from there on.

Well, in a way it is too bad that that wasn't the way it began, for it is more dramatic than the truth, making it seem that the manager of the club was an instrument of a benign fate that picked St. Peter's out of all the churches in that section for the special favors that Al and his friends had to offer. As a matter of fact, Father McCallion had known all along that one day the Governor of New York would appear in his church, for on New Year's Day of 1926, when Archbishop Walsh later to become Metropolitan of New Jersey but then Bishop of Trenton, sent him to the Pleasantville parish, almost his last words were:

"My friend, Governor Smith will be in Pleasantville sometime this spring. Be sure to take good care of him and see that he has every courtesy and consideration."

But the story itself, even with the imaginative beginning lopped off, is dramatic enough. It began, properly, on a Saturday night, or rather in the early hours of a Sunday morning, when a long and lively poker game was breaking up.

"I'm going to seven o'clock mass at St. Peter's, in Pleasantville," Al said. "Bishop Walsh tells me that's the nearest church."

He turned Bill Kenny, Jim Riordan, and Tim Mara.

"I know you're coming," he said. And to the others, who were non-Catholic:

"Even if you're not coming, you've got to kick in for the collection. Get it up now, before you go to bed, or I'll come around and get it from you in the morning."

Winners and losers alike threw their money on the table. Ten-dollar bills...twenties...fifties.

After but a few hours' sleep, Al, Kenny, Riordan, and Mara, their eyes still fogged by sleep, got up, dressed, and started downstairs. It was then that Riordan made a remark that Al repeated gleefully so many times its origin has been attributed to him. Looking in at one of the rooms where the others still lay, wrapped in slumber, Riordan said:

"Wouldn't it be awful if those fellows were right?"

Still chuckling, they left the club, got into a waiting car, and were driven to Pleasantville. Al later described the church as he first saw it:

"The parish property bordered on two dead end streets, one leading to a storage plant of the American Ice Company, the other to the freight station of the Pennsylvania Railroad. On the property, in the middle of an unimproved sandlot, was the church, made to seat about three hundred persons. There were but two masses on Sunday. Behind the church was a leftover barn which served the social demands of the parish. A lean-to on the back, which had been a chickencoop, became a kitchen. The room for the buggy became a place for suppers and dances and card parties. Hay was still in the loft when Father McCallion was tendered his reception."

After the mass in the little shingle-roofed church, the party met Father McCallion, who, although a young man, was well known in the diocese as priest, scholar, writer, editor, and teacher. They were greatly impressed with him and, having looked upon the scene of his struggle, made up their minds to help him. Most of them already were, or were to become, regular visitors to Sea View—the Smith family was to spend many summer week ends there and holidays all the year round—and their donations became the main financial support of the parish. Nor did Al solicit money only from the original group. He constantly brought new subscribers to church with him or collected from them at the Saturday night poker games or on the golf course.

Catholics, Protestants, Jews, or those of no faith whatever, including many who never saw St. Peter's, were appealed to by him, at Sea View or in New York or Albany or wherever he happened to meet them, and swelled the fund. One Jewish friend, Abram Akid, accompanied Al to mass one morning and left five hundred dollars with Father McCallion. On Easter Sunday of 1927, Al, Kenny, Riordan, Mara, William Todd, the shipbuilder, Dr. Arthur Leonard, and George Olvany each gave one hundred dollars. Mara laughingly offered to take the seven hundred to New York with him the next day and put it on a horse or buy stock with it, promising Father McCallion he would run it into a fortune, but the priest smilingly declined.

One Sunday morning Al gave Father McCallion five hundred dollars.

"That's from last night's game," he said.

Meeting the priest on the golf links on Monday morning, he gave him two hundred more.

"This is from a couple of fellows I missed Saturday night," he said. "They went to bed before I took up the collection and I didn't want to disturb them yesterday morning."

About that time Father McCallion had his picture taken with Al. The two were standing very close together and a friend, on seeing the picture, said:

"It looks as though the Governor were leaning on you."

"On the contrary," the priest said. "I'm leaning on him."

Once, when Al was leaving on a trip, he said to Father McCallion:

"If you need someone to dig up money for you when I'm away, call on this fellow."

He pointed to Orie Kelly.

"He knows where there's a lot of money," he added.

Kelly laughed, dug into his pocket and handed Father McCallion a hundred-dollar bill.

"That's to prove he isn't fooling, Father," he said. "When you need some more, let me know."

Bill Kenny not only gave his money freely but sent frequent shipments of choice food, particularly fruit from Florida and California, for the rectory and convent tables.

As the years went by, the money that Al either gave in person or raised among his friends made it possible for Father McCallion to tear down the ramshackle structures that Al had seen in 1926 and to replace them with a beautiful church, a lyceum, a rectory, and a convent for the teaching nuns. In the lyceum is the Governor Smith Room, and on the grounds a statue of St. Thomas More, Catholic statesman, legislator, and martyr. On one side of it is the inscription:

"The legal profession erects this monument as a lasting memorial to the Honorable Alfred Emanual Smith, orator.

legislator, leader of the laity, a founder in this parish, four times Governor of New York State, sometime candidate for president of the United States."

This was one case in which those who wished to erect a memorial to a man did not wait to do so until he had died. On November 26, 1937, when Mayor Scott M. Long of Pleasantville had declared a holiday, a great crowd gathered for the unveiling. Present were Al and his family and many of the friends who had given so willingly to the church. The Right Reverend Monsignor Spillane, Vicar General of Trenton, presided over the ceremonies and blessed the statue, which was unveiled by Al's grandson, Walter, Jr. Addresses were made by Governor Harold Hoffman of New Jersey and William J. Morrison, president of the New Jersey Bar Association.

In reply to the other speakers, who had heaped high praise upon him for his untiring efforts on behalf of the parish, Al disclaimed all credit for himself and his friends and gave it all to Father McCallion.

"Maybe what he says it right," a somewhat irreverent listener said, "for Father McCallion has done a grand job. But all the same, a lot of people around here are calling St. Peter's 'The Smithsonian Institute.'"

28: A DECLARATION OF FAITH

IN 1927 A SWEEP OF RELIGIOUS AND RACIAL IN-
tolerance that had the country in its unholy grip had
not yet reached its peak. That would come a year later, sully-
ing the national election and saddening the decent and
thoughtful members of all faiths. But by 1927 the Ku Klux
Klan was on the march in great strength, wielding the lash
and the tar brush, its hooded face lighted by the fiery cross,
as Catholic, Jew, and Negro were hunted and scourged. In
Augusta, Georgia, when a visiting priest from New York,
hacking his way around a golf course, asked his little Negro
caddy if he were a Catholic, the boy shook his head and
asked, bitterly:

"Ain't it bad enough to be a Nigger down here?"

Now a Catholic had the presidential nomination of his
party at arm's length, and a campaign of unrivaled, almost
unbelievable abuse had been launched to thwart him. Scur-
rilous pamphlets, anonymous letters, behind-the-hand whis-
perings, employing all the old familiar lies and many new
ones, devilishly concocted, were used against him, and Adna
Wright Leonard, a bishop of the Methodist church, thundered:

"No governor who kisses the Papal ring can come within
gunshot of the White House!"

Now the issue was cracked wide open. The April issue of
the *Atlantic Monthly* carried a letter addressed to Al Smith
which, on release by the magazine, was reprinted in all the
important newspapers of the country. It was written by
Charles C. Marshall, hitherto unheard of but described as a

retired attorney, a student of church law, and an Episco-
palian, and it challenged, on religious grounds, Smith's qualifications for the presidency. The burden of his reasoning
was that a Catholic must be answerable to the dictates of his
church in any matter that seemed to bring the church and
the state into conflict, and that the more conscientious a
Catholic he was, the more likely he would be to accept that
dictation without question.

Smith had known of the letter before it appeared in the
public prints. A proof of it had been sent by Ellery Sedgwick,
the editor of the magazine, to Franklin D. Roosevelt with
the suggestion that some friend of the Governor's, perhaps
Roosevelt himself, reply to it, and adding an assurance that
full space for the reply would be granted by the *Atlantic*.
Roosevelt sent the letter to Smith who, never one to want
another to fight his battles, said:

"I'll answer it myself."

Since the letter dealt with theology and the enunciation
of canonical law and since Al was neither a theologian nor a
lawyer, he sought counsel on those points from two of his
closest friends, Father Francis J. Duffy, famous chaplain of
the Sixty-ninth Regiment and a former professor of theology,
and Justice Joseph M. Proskauer. Aided only by their clari-
fication of the points raised by Marshall and the technically
proper answers to them, he wrote his reply with characteristic
honesty and vigor, basing it on his record in public life and
concluding with this ringing declaration:

"I summarize my creed as an American Catholic. I believe
in the worship of God according to the faith and practice of
the Roman Catholic Church. I recognize no power in the
institutions of my Church to interfere with the operations
of the Constitution of the United States or the enforcement
of the law of the land. I believe in absolute freedom of conscience for all men and in equality of all churches, all sects
and all beliefs before the law as a matter of right and not as
a matter of favor. I believe in the absolute separation of

church and state and in the strict enforcement of the pro-
visions of the Constitution that Congress shall make no law
respecting an establishment of religion or prohibiting the
free exercise thereof/I believe that no tribunal of any church
has any power to make any decree of any force in the law of
the land, other than to establish the status of its own com-
municants within its own church. I believe in the support of
the public school as one of the corner-stones of American
liberty. I believe in the right of every parent to choose
whether his child shall be educated in the public school or in
a religious school supported by those of his own faith. I
believe in the principle of non-interference by this country
in the internal affairs of other nations and that we should
stand steadfastly against any such interference by whomsoever
it may be urged. And I believe in the common brotherhood of
man under the common fatherhood of God.

/"In this spirit I join with fellow Americans of all creeds
in a fervent prayer that never again in this land will any
public servant be challenged because of the faith in which
he has tried to walk humbly with God." /

His words gave pause to, but could not stop for long, the
tide that was running against him. They were warmly applauded by the newspapers, and public speakers gave new
impetus to them by repeating them as a confession of faith
by one who would sacrifice no shred of his religious belief
for political advancement. But from those who assailed him
they brought only obscene laughter, and the tide rolled on
until, one day, it engulfed him.

The presidential campaign was a year and more away, yet
everyone, Democrat and Republican alike, was looking at
Alfred E. Smith. His increasingly impressive record as governor, his frequent and outspoken contempt of the Klan,
and his attitude toward Prohibition made him, in the eyes of
the Democrats, the man on whom they must pin their hopes
in 1928, and in the eyes of the Republicans the most dan-

gerous threat to the continuance of their party in national power.

Made acutely aware of this by constant references to him in the newspapers as the inevitable Democratic standard-bearer and by the growing number of political leaders from all over the country who called on him, he remained faithfully at his desk in Albany and resisted all attempts to induce him to make forays out of the state for the purpose of showing himself anew to the voters. He clung to the notion, quaint though it seemed to some of his advisers, that the people of New York had elected him for the fourth time to run their state government and not to go stumping about the country adding personally to the buildup that already was under way with no help from him.

Judge Proskauer, Mrs. Moskowitz, and Bob Moses, now his Secretary of State, were in agreement with him, yet once they saw a chance to get him out, believing that, in the circumstances, no criticism could be made of him. It was July and the governors of the nation were about to hold their annual conference at Portland, Maine, and Mrs. Moskowitz suggested that he attend, believing that for him to do so could do him no harm and might do him some good.

"No," he said, firmly.

"Why?"

"I'm too busy."

"You could get away for a few days. Bob could run things in your absence. You know he'd do it all right, don't you?"

"Yes."

"Then you'll go?"

"No," he said again.

"But why not?"

"Emily's going to have her baby this month. I've got to stay here for that."

Mrs. Moskowitz laughed.

"Who are you, the doctor?" she asked.

He didn't think that was funny.

"Never mind," he said. "I'm not going to leave her at a time like this."

Mrs. Moskowitz knew there was no arguing with him once he had made up his mind. She threw up her hands and walked from the room. Encountering Emily a little later, she said:

"We could kill you."

Emily was startled.

"Who's 'we'?"

"Judge Proskauer and Bob and I."

"Why?"

"We think it would be a good idea for your father to go to the governors' conference, but he refused to go. And do you know the reason?"

"No."

"Because you're going to have your baby this month!"

Emily shrugged.

"You know Father," she said.

So the Governor remained in Albany. The baby, a girl, was born on July 25 and was christened Mary. Arthur had two boys, Walter and Arthur, but this was the Governor's first grandaughter. Moreover, she was born in Albany and he could see her every day and he was devoted to her.

After the turn of the year, the preliminary campaign that had been launched for him increased in tempo. Increased, too, was the number of persons who thronged to Albany to see him. Many of these were old and close friends, rallying strongly about him, eager to do everything they could to help him and seeking to learn from him just what he wanted them to do. Others were county and state chairmen of the party. Still others were visitors to the state capital who would not leave without at least a glimpse of him or a handshake or a word or two of greeting.

Among the new and influential supporters he had gained was John J. Raskob, chairman of the board of General Motors, who hitherto had had no political affiliations and was unknown to Smith except by reputation. Raskob, however, was a great admirer of Smith's, and his interest in the man was quickened by association with some of his close friends, particularly Bill Kenny and Terence McManus, the latter a New York lawyer. At that time, Raskob, Kenny, and McManus all had sons in the Newman School in New Jersey, and McManus had organized a Father's Club dedicated to the interests of the undergraduate body. At the first meeting, held at the school, McManus was elected president in recognition of the fact that the project was his idea, and Kenny proposed that the next meeting be marked by a dinner in his Tiger Room, atop his office building in New York.

On the night of the dinner, McManus, seated next to Kenny at the head table, saw Raskob sitting unobtrusively at one end of the U of tables stretched before them and said to Kenny:

"There's Raskob sitting away down there. Let's get him up here."

Neither of them knew Raskob well, and Kenny asked: "Why?"

"Well, he seems like a very nice fellow," McManus said, "and as he doesn't know many of us, I thought it would be nice to ask him to sit between you and me."

"All right," Kenny said. "Get him up here."

Raskob, now seated next to Kenny, soon was engaged in conversation with him on the subject of Al Smith.

"They were so intent," McManus has said, "that they all but forgot the purpose of the dinner."

It was right after that that Raskob aligned himself with the inner circle of Smith's friends and advisers, and by his generous contributions to the campaign gave very tangible testimony of his faith in the man. And so the Smith movement gained in prestige and money as Houston, Texas, was set as the site for the convention to be held in June.

29: TIME OUT FOR LAUGHS

ALTHOUGH UNALTERABLY OPPOSED TO LEAVing the state during this period, Al made frequent weekend trips to New York, where the Biltmore still served as his "town house." There were many pleasant gatherings there, and the Smiths would dine on the roof with their friends or other members of the family, and the high light of these occasions always came when Al and Mrs. Smith waltzed together. Then the floor would be cleared as the other dancers stood around to watch and applaud, for they danced beautifully. There were dinners elsewhere, and affairs such as the Emerald Ball, which they had attended faithfully for years, and there were, as always, laughs for the Governor.

As sort of court jester in those days he had the always amusing Tim Lyons who was—and still is—a deputy county clerk in Brooklyn, but is best known for his specialty as an impersonator, for fun, of a Norwegian. Stocky, bald-headed, spectacled, dead-panned, possessed of an authentic Scandinavian accent and a master of double talk, for years he has been causing confusion when turned loose upon the unsuspecting as a captain of the Norwegian Army, an admiral of the Norwegian Navy, or in some cases as a Norwegian diplomat visiting this country for the first time. Al first met him at a stag party at the New York Athletic Club where, under the aegis of Christy Bohnsack, newspaperman and publicist and an old friend of Smith's, he has enjoyed some of his greatest triumphs. Completely taken in by Tim on that first occasion, and hugely enjoying the joke even though it was on him, Al had a great deal of fun with him thereafter at the expense of his friends.

Mrs. Smith's first encounter with him was at a political gathering at Borough Hall in Brooklyn one night during the 1926 campaign when the Governor couldn't resist the opportunity to tease her. Spying Tim in the group on the steps of the hall, he took him aside when Mrs. Smith was engaged in conversation with some of her friends.

"Give Mrs. Smith a full treatment," he said.

Tim was hesitant, fearing Mrs. Smith might be offended, but Al said:

"Don't worry. She'll love it when she finds out it is a gag."

A few moments later, while Al purposefully remained away from his wife's side, Tim approached her and said:

"Hello, Katie."

Mrs. Smith, surprised at his greeting but thinking perhaps he was a politician whom she had met and should know, smiled and said:

"Oh! Good evening. How are you?"

"Fine," Tim said.

That was the last word she understood. Utterly confused by his heavy accent and the mumble-jumble of double talk, realizing now and then that he was asking her a question but totally unable to answer him, she was red-faced and stammering when Al rejoined her.

"Hello," he said. "Who's your friend?"

Mrs. Smith didn't know, which added to her embarrassment. Tim, bowing to Al, introduced himself as Captain Olsen of the Norwegian Army. Al gravely acknowledged the introduction and shook hands with him.

"I have been trying to tell Mrs. Smith," he said, clearly, "that ..."

He turned to her and resumed his double talk

She looked helplessly at Al, who apparently was following Tim's words closely and nodding in agreement. Tim turned to him.

"You understand me, do you not?" he asked.

"Perfectly," Al said.

"Good. Now, Mrs. Smith—"

Mrs. Smith's embarrassment was rapidly taking her to the verge of panic when Al, roaring with laughter, called Tim off and properly introduced him. As Al had said, Mrs. Smith joined them in laughter when she realized it was a joke, and thoroughly enjoyed Tim's subsequent adventures among their friends.

One night in April of 1928 the Governor and Mrs. Smith attended a full dress review at one of the armories in New York, and Al informed the colonel of the regiment, whom he had known for years, that he had taken the liberty of asking a friend of his, Admiral Olsen of the Norwegian Navy, to join him at the reception that followed the review. The Colonel said he would be delighted to meet the Admiral and told his adjutant to have a group of officers meet the distinguished visitor at the door and escort him to the room where the reception would be held.

When the review was over and the reception was in progress, Tim—in evening clothes and with a broad red ribbon across his shirt front—was ushered into the room. Al, saying, "Ah! Here he is!" walked to meet him—and was almost knocked down by the Colonel in his eagerness to greet the Admiral. There was saluting and bowing on all sides as the Admiral was presented to the Colonel, the members of his staff, and the others present—and a few minutes later the room was seething with suppressed anger and indignation as Tim the Admiral, without resorting to double talk this time but speaking so loudly and clearly that everybody could hear him, compared the American military establishments, with special emphasis on the New York National Guard, to the Norwegian Army and Navy, blandly giving the Americans a terrific going-over. Only when it seemed that the officers no longer would be able to restrain themselves did Al turn their indignation to laughter by revealing the true identity of the Admiral.

On another occasion, a week or so later, he introduced Tim to a distinguished New York jurist and a bulwark of the Democratic party as Mr. Olsen, president of the Norwegian-American Line; and Tim, having warmed up the victim for a while, invited him, his family, and any friends he might care to include in the party, on a trip to Norway.

"You shall be my guests from the time we leave New York until we return." Tim beamed. "You will come, will you not?"

The jurist was delighted. Of course he would go.

"Good!" Tim said. "We will sail the first week in June and return—oh, sometime in July."

Swept away by the prospect, the victim completely missed the significance of the time set for the trip.

"Wonderful!" he said. "Thanks so much! I must tell my wife!"

But the first one he told was the Governor.

"That's great. I know you'll enjoy it," Al said. Then: "Too bad you'll be away during the convention."

"What!" the jurist yelled. "I never thought of that! I must tell Mr. Olsen I can't go."

He rushed after Mr. Olsen.

"I'm very sorry," he said, "but I will be unable to go on that trip."

Mr. Olsen looked at him coldly.

"So?" he said. "But you have already accepted my invitation."

"I know. But that is the time of the Democratic convention at Houston in which, we hope, Governor Smith will be nominated for the presidency."

Mr. Olsen's tone was even icier.

"Regardless of your reasons," he said, "in my country I am not accustomed to having my invitations at first accepted and then rejected by a magistrate."

The other's face flamed.

"I am not a magistrate!" he snapped. "I am a justice of the Supreme Court!"

"And what, pray, does that mean?"

The hapless victim explained to him the eminence and dignity of his position. Tim diabolically made the explanation difficult for him by pretending not to understand him, finally turning in feigned impatience to Jim Kelly, another court clerk from Brooklyn, whom he previously had introduced as his secretary and interpreter. Some gibberish passed between them and Kelly said to the jurist:

"I am sorry, but Mr. Olsen does not quite understand you."

Then to Tim, more gibberish. And to the jurist:

"I have told him that you are a justice of the Supreme Court, which in this country is a high honor. That you are a man greatly looked up to by the people, who have a very high regard for your intelligence."

"Thank you."

More gibberish from Tim.

"And what does he say?"

"He says," Kelly reported, "that in that case you have even less excuse than a magistrate would have for offending a guest in your country, which he thinks is very bad because he understands that in this country magistrates are known to be very low things."

Just when it appeared that the Justice of the Supreme Court—who once had been a magistrate himself—was about to wind up and take a punch at Mr. Olsen, Al stepped in and averted possible bloodshed.

30: NOMINATED FOR THE PRESIDENCY

IN ALBANY, THINGS WERE HUMMING. BESIDES the regular business of the state, to which the Governor continued to apply himself, there were numerous conferences with his advisers, including Van Namee, who shortly was to go to Houston to set up the Smith headquarters, and morning and afternoon meetings with some forty newspaper correspondents who had arrived from all sections of the country.

One night when the Warners were at dinner at the mansion, Bob Moses called the Major on the telephone. When the Major returned to the room, he said to the Governor:

"To counteract some silly talk about you appointing only Democrats and Catholics to jobs, Bob is getting up a list showing that many of your appointments have gone to Republicans and men of other faiths, such as himself. He wants to know what I am. What shall I tell him?"

The Governor never had discussed politics with his Superintendent of Police and son-in-law.

"What are you?" he asked.

Slightly embarrassed, Warner said:

"A Republican."

Smith laughed.

"Well, go tell him," he said. "The fact that I've got an outlander right in my own family will make the report look better."

The week before the convention, Catherine Smith was married to Francis Quillinan in the Cathedral of the Im-

maculate Conception, in Albany. Coming at that time, the
wedding attracted a tremendous crowd, and so many members of the family and their friends descended upon the
mansion that in the excitement even the approaching test at
Houston was forgotten for a couple of days.

When quiet had been restored, Mrs. Smith and the young
Smiths, with the exception of Emily, set out for Houston as
the guests of Bill Kenny. The strategy agreed upon was that
Al not attend the convention, and Emily and her husband
remained at Albany to keep him company.

Van Namee and his other friends had done their work exceedingly well. The expected struggle at Houston did not
materiaize and Al was nominated on the first ballot. Victory
had come with the suddenness of a one-round knockout in
the prize ring, and the excitement at Houston was duplicated
at Albany. A great crowd had gathered about the mansion,
awaiting the flash from Texas. When it came, the crowd
poured through the doors, swirled through the great halls
and engulfed everyone in sight, from the Governor to the
last dazed, bewildered state trooper in the detail that John
Warner had posted. Because of the difference in time between Texas and New York, it was then three o'clock in the
morning. Dawn was breaking over the town when the well-
wishers, gently nudged by the troopers and city policemen,
finally dispersed. Quite exhausted but almost deliriously
happy, Al and Emily and Major Warner talked with Mrs.
Smith and the rest of the family on the telephone and then
sat down to a breakfast of bacon and eggs before retiring.

Exciting as that had been, it was only the beginning. Never
before had Al Smith known such a time as he was to have in
the next few months as he campaigned against Herbert
Hoover, nominated by the Republicans when Coolidge, in
his own words, did not choose to run. Every day, every hour
was crowded as in Albany . . . New York . . . Omaha . . . Oklahoma City . . . up and down and across the country . . . he
waged a gallant fight for the principles in which he believed.

Now and then counselors advised him not to say this or not to say that, since by saying this or that he might offend this one or that. But he brushed aside this advice, well meant and politically wise though it might have been. He would say what was in his heart, believing that it was better to invite defeat by his honesty than to be elected on a platform of subterfuge.

31: A GALLANT CAMPAIGN LOST

JOHN RASKOB, IN SPITE OF HIS LACK OF POLITical experience, was named by Smith as chairman of the national committee, with Van Namee to do the spadework. Al felt that this combination, with Raskob at the head of the group to impress the businessmen and Van Namee applying his political wisdom, acquired over the years, to the actual direction of the campaign, would be most effective.

Following the official notification of his nomination, a ceremony which took place, most appropriately, in the Assembly Chamber at Albany where he had spent so many happy years, Smith set forth in his speech of acceptance the principles on which he would seek election. These, for the most part, were the principles which he had espoused as governor and which he now wished to see adopted by the nation:

Reorganization and consolidation of government bureaus that would lead to a more efficient, truly economic administration.

A Prohibition law that would breed temperance and eliminate corruption in national, state, and civic law-enforcement bodies.

A sound agricultural program that would afford needed relief to hard-pressed farmers.

Conservation of water power and its control by the people, not by private interests.

Laws to protect the wages, working and living conditions, health and general social betterment of the nation's breadwinners and their families.

Revision of the tariff law to take it out of politics.

Better relations with foreign powers, with special emphasis on the South American republics.

He had put himself squarely on record as to the things for which he stood. As always, he had spoken freely, boldly, with no qualifying phrases. Now he was ready to go before the country, and a few days later he began the speaking tour that had been mapped out for him by the committee. With him went Mrs. Smith, his son Alfred, his daughters, his nephew, John Glynn; Bill Kenny, Mrs. Caroline O'Day, General Charles W. Berry, Major General William N. Haskell, Norman H. Davis, Judge Bernard L. Shientag, and Judge Proskauer. Bob Moses remained in Albany to run the state government.

Ahead of Smith went Charlie Hand and Christy Bohnsack, to handle the advance publicity and to see that all details of the arrangements for his coming had been carried out. Omaha was the first stop, and Bohnsack, arriving two days before the candidate, found a marathon dance in progress in the auditorium where he was to speak.

"How long has this been going on?" he asked the manager of the hall.

"Two weeks."

"Well," said Christy, a very forthright and outspoken young man, "get the bums out."

"But I can't," the manager protested. "They are scheduled to continue until Thursday afternoon."

"Thursday afternoon! Why, the Governor is speaking here Thursday night. How are you going to air the place out and get it ready that quickly?"

The manager shrugged.

"I'll have to do the best I can," he said.

"Listen," Christy said, "there is only one thing for you to do. That is to have them out of here by tonight or tomorrow morning at the latest. You knew the Governor was coming and you shouldn't have let the thing run so long."

The manager pleaded for more time, but Christy was obdurate.

"All right," he said. "They'll be out by tomorrow morning."

But on the morrow the band still wailed and sobbed and the weary dancers dragged themselves listlessly about.

"Well?" Christy demanded.

"They insist upon finishing," the manager said. "So I thought it would be all right if we put them under the stage and let them finish there."

Christy looked at him in amazement.

"Do you mean to tell me that you seriously are thinking of having a candidate for the presidency of the United States talking from a stage with a marathon dance going on under his feet?" he asked.

"Sure," the manager said. "What's wrong about that?"

Christy went to a telephone and called the chief of police, with whom he had been going over the arrangements for handling the crowds at the railroad station and the hall.

"Come up here right away," he said. "I want you to do something."

When the chief arrived, Christy said:

"Throw those tramps out."

"But he can't do that!" the manager said. "This show is billed—"

"I don't care what it's billed for!" Christy yelled. "Out they go—or I'll wire the Governor immediately not to come here!"

He was bluffing, of course. Radio and other commitments demanded that the Governor speak in Omaha on the appointed date. But the bluff worked. The dancers were shooed out and when Smith and his party arrived, everything was in readiness for the candidate.

Christy told Al about the manager's plan to have the marathon dance continue under the stage, and Al laughed.

"That would have been a novelty," he said.

From Omaha, Al went to Oklahoma City. It had been impressed upon him, in his journey from Nebraska through Kansas and into Oklahoma, that the main question in the minds of the voters he would address in that part of the country concerned his religion.

"I'll answer it," he said, grimly. "I'll drag all the things they have been muttering and whispering right out in the open. We'll bring this thing to a showdown right here in Oklahoma City."

Those about him cautioned him to do nothing of the sort. They were sure that plain speaking on his part would accomplish nothing for his own good and might harm him greatly. Even Mrs. Moskowitz, who had remained in New York with Van Namee to direct the national publicity from there but to whom he spoke on the telephone every night, added her voice to those that were raised against his. But he was determined to speak out, even though to do so might cost him the presidency.

His speech was one of the most memorable ever made in a political campaign. Fighting mad, fearing no one, and pulling no punches, he ripped and tore into his enemies, calling them by name, striking them down, affirming his faith, denouncing those who had said, openly or covertly, that because he was a Catholic he should be barred from the White House.

His first target was a member of his own party, former Senator Owen of Oklahoma, who had said he would not support Smith because of his Tammany affiliations.

"Senator Owen and his kind are not sincere," Al thundered. "They know that this Tammany cry is an attempt to drag a red herring across the trail.

"I know what lies behind all this and I shall tell you. I specifically refer to the question of my religion. Ordinarily, that word should never be used in a political campaign. The necessity for using it is forced upon me by Senator Owen and his kind and I feel that at least once in this campaign, I, as the candidate of the Democratic party, owe it to the people of

The Ovation Given Al Smith during the 1928 Presidential Campaign

The Governor and Mrs. Smith Look Out over the City They Loved

this country to discuss frankly and openly with them this attempt of Senator Owen and the forces behind him to inject bigotry, hatred, intolerance, and un-American sectarian division into a campaign which should be an intelligent debate of the important issues which confront the American people....

"The Grand Dragon of the Realm of Arkansas, writing to a citizen of that state, urges my defeat because I am a Catholic and in the letter suggests to the man, who happened to be a delegate to the Democratic convention, that by voting against me he was upholding American ideals and institutions as established by our forefathers. The Grand Dragon that has thus advised a delegate to the national convention to vote against me because of my religion is a member of an order known as the Ku Klux Klan, who have the effrontery to refer to themselves as one hundred per cent Americans. Yet they are totally ignorant of the history and tradition of this country and its institutions and, in the name of Americanism, they breathe into the hearts and souls of their members hatred of millions of their fellow countrymen because of their religious belief.

"Nothing could be so out of line with the spirit of America. Nothing could be so foreign to the teachings of Jefferson. Nothing could be so contradictory of our whole history. Nothing could be so false to the teachings of our Divine Lord Himself....

"As contemptible as anything could possibly be is an article on the very front page of a publication devoted to the doings of a church wherein the gospel of Christ is preached. I refer to the *Ashland Avenue Baptist,* a publication coming from Lexington, Kentucky, in which a bitter and cruel attack is made upon me personally and is so ridiculous that ordinarily no attention should be paid to it. It speaks of me driving an automobile down Broadway at the rate of fifty miles on hour, and specially states I was driving the car myself while intoxicated. Everybody who knows me knows full well I do not know how to drive an automobile, that I never tried it. As for the rest of the contemptible, lying statement, it is as false as this part."

Declaring his belief that Republicans high in the councils of their party encouraged the distortions that were being whispered, shouted, and printed about him, he continued:

"Giving them the benefit of all reasonable doubt, they at least remain silent on the exhibition that Mrs. Willebrandt made of herself before the Ohio Conference of the Methodist Episcopal Church when she said:

" 'There are two thousand pastors here. You have in your church more than six hundred thousand members of the Methodist Church in Ohio alone. This is enough to swing the election. The six hundred thousand have friends in other states. Write to them.'

"Mrs. Willebrandt holds a place of prominence in the Republican administration in Washington; she is an assistant attorney general of the United States. By silence, after such a speech, the only inference one can draw is that the administration approves such political tactics. Mrs. Willebrandt is not an irresponsible person. She was chairman of the Committee on Credentials in the Republican National Convention at Kansas City.

"What would be the effect upon these same people if a prominent official of the government of the State of New York under me suggested to a gathering of the pastors of my church that they do for me what Mrs. Willebrandt suggests be done for Hoover? . . .

"I here emphatically declare that I do not wish any member of my faith in any part of the United States to vote for me on religious grounds. I want them to vote for me only when in their hearts and consciences they become convinced that my election will promote the best interests of our country. By the same token, I cannot refrain from saying that any person who votes against me simply because of my religion is not, to my way of thinking, a good citizen.

"Let me remind the Democrats of this country that we belong to the party of Thomas Jefferson, whose proudest boast was that he was the author of the Virginia statute for religious freedom. Let me remind the citizens of every political faith that that statute of religious freedom has become a part of the sacred heritage of our land. The constitutional guaranty that there should be no religious test for public office is not a mere form of words. It represents the most vital principle that ever was given any people.

"I attack those who seek to undermine it, not only because I am a good Christian but because I am a good American and a product of America and of American institutions. Everything I am and everything I hope to be I owe to those institutions.

"The absolute separation of State and Church is part of the fundamental basis of our Constitution. I believe in that separation and in all that it implies. That belief must be a part of the fundamental faith of every true American. Let the people of this country decide this election upon the great and real issues of the campaign and upon nothing else."

Most of the country, thrilled by his speech, acclaimed him for his honesty and courage, but in those sections where narrowness and bigotry were strong the dark mutterings continued. From a political standpoint, the speech had been made in vain, but at least it had cleared the air and it had satisfied him, right down to the roots of his rugged soul.

He moved on. Denver . . . Helena, Montana . . . Butte . . . Minneapolis . . . St. Paul . . . Milwaukee—where he lashed out boldly against Prohibition and all its works, with emphasis on the crime it had spawned . . . and then to Rochester, where the Democratic state convention was to be held.

The selection of a candidate to succeed him as governor concerned him greatly. His own choice was Franklin D. Roosevelt. Roosevelt, however, was showing no inclination to accept the nomination. Aware, a few weeks earlier, that he was being seriously considered, Roosevelt left his home in

Hyde Park for Warm Springs, Georgia, and on his departure said to Van Namee:

"If you hear anybody talking about me for governor, you can tell them that I do not want the job."

Van Namee, meeting Smith in Rochester, repeated what Roosevelt had said. Al, however, believed that Roosevelt could be induced to run if he were approached properly, and held out for him in the councils to decide on names to be presented to the convention, against those whose wagons were hitched to other candidates or believed that Roosevelt would not weaken in his stand. Efforts to get Roosevelt on the telephone failed, and it was only when the aid of Mrs. Roosevelt was obtained that he was persuaded to come to the telephone and, after a lengthy conversation with members of the nominating committee, agreed to allow his name to be presented.

He was nominated, and as headquarters for his campaign were being set up in New York, he asked a favor of Smith: Would Al let him have Van Namee as his campaign manager? Van Namee was extremely valuable to Smith and already had his hands full at the national headquarters, but Al was willing to have him direct Roosevelt if it would not put too much of a burden on him. It was agreeable to Van Namee to work for Roosevelt, too, and it was so arranged.

The convention over and his choice nominated, Smith took to the road again. Nashville ... Louisville, where someone turned the steam heat on in the hall where Al spoke, although it was a warm night, and where someone else spread a fast-moving rumor that he was drunk ... Sedalia, Missouri, where Norman Davis' pocket was picked ... St. Louis and Chicago.

In Chicago a great crowd waited at the station, and as Al and Mrs. Smith left the train, the surging mob broke through police lines. It was with the greatest difficulty that a cordon of cops about the candidate and his wife got them to their automobile. The remainder of the party, jostled and pushed about in the wild scramble, sought to make their way through the hastily re-formed police lines to reach the cars.

Catherine, escorted by Bill Kenny, was stopped by a policeman.

"Get back," the cop said. "If you want to get out of the station, go around the other way. You can't go through here."

"But, officer, this is the Governor's daughter," Kenny said.

The cop seemed a trifle suspicious.

"Well, all right," he said, after a moment. "Go ahead."

A minute or so later Emily, with General Berry, struggled up to the same cop.

"We've got to get through," Berry said. "This young woman is the Governor's daughter."

The cop's laugh was scornful.

"Scram, brother," he said. "I already had that one pulled on me."

By the time Emily and Berry had talked their way out of the jam Al, who had refused to leave the station until both daughters were present or accounted for, was almost frantic, fearing they would be trampled upon. Thereafter, it was decided, when the party reached a town, Al and Mrs. Smith would be the last, not the first, to leave the train, so that the others might go unmolested to the line of cars.

From Chicago, Smith returned to Albany, spent a few days at work on legislative matters that awaited his attention, and then moved on to Boston. Here his greatest reception awaited him. Cheering crowds pressed all about him wherever he went, and two halls, other than that in which he spoke, were jammed with eager Democrats who listened to his speech over the radio.

"That was the night," Emily was to say later, "when we were all sure he would win, whatever doubts we might have felt in other parts of the country. It was hard to feel otherwise, with all those people yelling their heads off for him."

"I'll vote nine times for you, Al!" a man shouted at him. "O.K., pal," Al shouted back. "But don't get caught!"

Boston ... Providence ... Hartford ... Philadelphia ... Baltimore ... Brooklyn ... finally Madison Square Garden. The campaign was over. He had done all he could. He had spread his record and his program before the country. Far from dodging issues, he had rushed to meet them, sometimes ... as at Oklahoma City ... dragging them from the dark into the light. There wasn't a person who could hear or read who did not know all about him—who he was, where he came from, the influences that had helped to mold his life, the things for which he stood and the things he hoped to do.

And now there was nothing for him to do but to await the answer that would be given at the polls. Whatever it would be, he would abide by it. All he asked was that it be arrived at fairly, in justice not only to him but to the institutions of the republic.

It chanced that election day fell on November 6, which also was Mrs. Smith's birthday, and no matter what the outcome of the voting, Al was going to have a party for her as usual. And so a cake was baked and friends and relatives were invited for a midnight celebration at the Biltmore.

Al was listening to the returns at the gathering of the Tammany Society in the Sixty-ninth Regiment Armory when he knew, beyond all doubt, that he was defeated. From the beginning, there had been a depressing monotony about the reports from all sections of the country.

"Hoover carries ...

"The indications are that the county has given Hoover a plurality. ...

"Hoover sweeps the city of ...

"Hoover is gaining rapidly. ... Hoover has taken the lead. ... Hoover ... Hoover ... Hoover ..."

Now and then there would be a break. Massachusetts was running strongly for Smith. Rhode Island was in the Smith column. Smith was ahead in Georgia. Then the old hammering at his advances, however slight they may have been.

"Hoover . . . Hoover . . . Hoover . . . Hoover . . ."

He got up from his chair.

"Where are you going, Al?" someone asked.

"I'm going to the Biltmore," he said. "I want to tell Katie and the children and my sister, Mary."

One look at the faces of his wife and children and sister must have caused him to realize that he had nothing to tell them that they did not already know. But in defeat he wanted to be with them alone, as he had been with them so many times in victory. He gathered them about him in a room of the suite and, unnecessary as it must have seemed to him, he said:

"The returns are not all in yet, but I have lost. It cannot be helped. We did our best. We fought cleanly and I believe we fought well. And now, I don't want anybody to feel badly another moment. Remember," he said to the children, "the Our Father, which your mother and I taught you when you were little: 'Thy will be done on earth, as it is in heaven.'"

Mrs. Smith seemed relieved at the news of the defeat. Threats had been hurled against her husband in the underground newspapers of the violent anti-Catholic forces. His mail had been shot through with predictions that if he were elected he would be murdered even as he took the oath of office, no matter what safeguards were thrown about him. Unafraid himself, he had tried to keep a knowledge of these threats from her, but she had known of them, and as the campaign had reached its closing stages, her fears for him had increased. Now the danger of assassination had been removed from him.

"It is all for the best, I am sure," she said. "It is God's will."

"And now," Al said, the old heartiness in his voice again, "don't let's forget it's Mother's birthday! Bring on the cake and the ice cream!"

When the last vote was counted, it was seen that he had received over 15,000,000, but Hoover had triumphed with over 21,000,000. Smith had carried Alabama, Arkansas, Georgia, Louisiana, Massachusetts, Mississippi, Rhode Island, and South Carolina. He had not carried New York, a fact which undeniably hurt him, although Roosevelt had been elected governor.

There were, of course, a number of factors that had contributed to his defeat. One of these was the chicken-in-every-pot, two-cars-in-every-garage type of prosperity the country was enjoying, as Hoover had boasted. The stock market was having its greatest boom, millions were being made overnight by speculators, and all—on the surface—was so very right with the world that the odds were stacked against him from that angle. Even Prohibition was less irksome, as the busy bootleggers plied their trade—who cared if the flow of liquor was controlled by hoodlums and gangsters, and that lawlessness raked the land?

And yet, as state and party lines were broken and the Solid South caved in under the weight of prejudice, he could not help but believe that the decisive factor was his religion. That while he might not have won in any circumstance, he had had no chance to win because he was a Catholic.

32: "HOW COULD A BITTER MAN—"

HE WAS BITTER AFTER 1928, THEY SAID OF HIM in later years, those who did not know him.

"Bitter?" his friends have said, scornfully. "How could a bitter man do the things he did, live as he lived and give so much pleasure to those about him?"

The weight of the evidence lies clearly on the side of his friends. Saddened he undoubtedly was, but by the causes of his defeat and not the defeat itself. But he was not embittered, and having accepted defeat philosophically, he pressed on briskly, entering new fields, making new friends, enjoying himself wherever he went, completely happy in the love and companionship of his wife, his children, and his children's children.

In need of rest, he went to Biloxi, Mississippi, with Raskob, Kenny, and a few other friends, but his stay there was brief and he returned to Albany to take up again for the last time the duties of governor, which he would relinquish on the first of the new year. No victor, returning from his triumph, ever was more wildly hailed than he was when he stepped from the train, and once more he marched through cheering crowds to the mansion.

The month of December was a pleasant one. There was work to do but he tackled it energetically, sometimes moving so fast that it was difficult for his secretarial staff to keep pace with him. And at the end of every day's work, on his way to the mansion he unfailingly stopped off at the Warners' to see little Mary, now seventeen months old. More often than not he was accompanied on these visits by friends or state officials who had been in his office at closing time.

"Come on," he would say. "I want you to see my granddaughter."

Mary would have been put to bed by the time he arrived, but it was idle for her parents to suppose that she would go to sleep without seeing him. Anyone else could walk up the stairs that led to her bedroom without getting the slightest attention from her, but as soon as he put foot on the stairs, she would call out to him, struggling to her feet in her crib, her arms outstretched as she waited for him.

No one ever knew—Mrs. Smith or Harry Whitehead or the Governor himself—how many there would be for dinner on any given night. It was as it always had been wherever he was, and always would be:

"Come up to the house for dinner. Sure, it will be all right. Katie is expecting you."

Katie might not even be aware that the guest—or guests— were in town but that didn't make any difference to him nor to Katie either. There was always room for one more at the table . . . or three or four or seven. And several nights a week there would be motion pictures in the mansion. Animal pictures or comedies, of course.

The last Christmas in the mansion was one of the happiest of all. As always, Al had done most of the planning and most of the shopping, especially for the children. There was a huge tree from the Adirondacks, and stockings were hung before a wide fireplace for Mary Warner and Arthur's two small sons, and there were carols and old-time songs and a family party that would have warmed the heart of Charles Dickens.

On New Year's Day, Al Smith placed the government of the state in the hands of Franklin Delano Roosevelt, and as soon as the inauguration of the new governor was completed, he left for New York. On his arrival, he was happily surprised to find that the Sixty-ninth Regiment, which had marched in his honor in Albany in 1919, was drawn up before the Grand Central Station to greet him.

There was a rumor in political circles, which soon was to be confirmed, not by a direct public admission on the part of either man but by the fact that neither took the trouble to deny it, that a coolness had developed between Smith and his successor, whose nomination he had engineered. The story was that Smith, seeking to make things easy as possible for Roosevelt by coaching him in the days between his election and his inauguration, however unwittingly, had been too solicitous to suit the new encumbent.

"Frank is resentful of Al's big-brotherly attitude," a friend of both said at the time. "He appreciates all Al did for him, but now he wants to assert himself. In other words, he wants everybody to know that he is governor on his own and that, free of Smith's influence, he is capable of running the state the way it should be run."

Certainly Roosevelt, whatever the reason that prompted him to do so, rejected Smith's recommendations on numerous appointments and was more than a little obvious about putting a distance between himself and those who had been close to Smith.

Among those who left Albany—and politics—with Al was Mrs. Moskowitz. She had labored for him, and the ideas he represented, with great zeal, and his defeat in the presidential campaign had been a sorry blow to her, who had visioned him one day in the White House.

Those who had voted against him were dismissed by her with the observation:

"They just were not educated up to him."

But at least for the present, all things political were behind Smith. They would catch up with him again. But now he was free to go where he would, to do as he pleased.

"Your husband is among the unemployed," he had said

gaily to Mrs. Smith as they rode down from Albany on the first of January.

"That's awful," she said, laughing. "How does it feel?"

"Great!" he said. "Let's go places and have fun. Where do you want to go?"

"Any place you say," she said. "You know that."

It was cold in New York and the South beckoned. Palm trees and sunlit beaches and soft winds. Palm Beach... Miami ... the west coast of Florida ... Havana.

"How does that sound to you?" he asked.

"Fine," she said. "When do we start?"

"As soon as we get the trunks and bags packed."

They had an even better time than they had expected. At Miami, Al spent a pleasant afternoon with Hoover, who had gone there for a rest before assuming his duties at Washington, the presidential inauguration at that time still being scheduled not in January but on March 4. At Sarasota, as the guest of John Ringling, he had the run of the winter quarters of the circus, a privilege which no small boy could have enjoyed to a greater extent. Overcoming his distaste for travel by water, he was thrilled by the boat trip from Miami to Havana and was entranced by the old Cuban city. This was his first visit to a foreign shore, and he found it exciting.

Back in this country, new honors awaited him. The University of Notre Dame conferred upon him the Laetare Medal, awarded annually to the Catholic layman who, in his field, achieved the greatest distinction reflecting credit on the Roman Catholic faith, and Manhattan College gave him an LL.D. He was invited to speak before a group of faculty members at Harvard University, and, simply by being natural and discoursing with great clarity on subjects familiar to him, he impressed his audience to such a degree that Professor Whitehead, one of the most learned and distinguished among them, exclaimed:

"How Aristotle would have liked this address! Why

shouldn't Harvard make Al Smith professor of political science?"

He also ceased to be one of the unemployed. He wrote his autobiography, *Up to Now,* which was first published in the *Saturday Evening Post* and later was brought out in book form by the Viking Press. He became a director of the Metropolitan Life, the New York Life (where, four years or so later, he was joined by Hoover), the County Trust Company, and other banking or insurance firms. He was chairman of the board of the Y.M.C.A. and a member of the board of the Beekman Street Hospital. The brown derby was being hung in strange places.

His writings, however, claimed most of his time from March to September. In addition to completing his autobiography he contributed a series of weekly articles on politics to the McNaught Syndicate that appeared in the New York *World* and many other newspapers. He was, for a time, an editor of the *New Outlook.*

This was a rather curious turn in the life of one who never had been a student in school and who seldom had been known to read a book. But he had something to say and knew how to say it clearly. All his life he had been a great listener, going to people rather than to books for his information, and soaking up that information and storing it away in his retentive memory. Trained as a speaker, he knew that to put his ideas across he must couch them in the simplest and most direct words. Thus his writings had substance and value and were easily understood, even by those not well informed politically.

As a matter of fact, his writings really were talks, for he dictated his autobiography and all his newspaper articles, and any rough edges that showed up in the transcript of his words were knocked off by Mrs. Moskowitz, who had formed her own publicity bureau in New York. To take his dictation, Mrs. Moskowitz engaged a young woman named Mary Carr, who had been her secretary in the Democratic headquarters during the campaign. Mary had seen Smith only once and was in great awe of him, but he soon put her at her ease and she found working with him quite the most pleasant job she had had in her brief career—she was only a couple of years out of a secretarial school.

In September, Al accepted a position that he was to hold for the rest of his life. On the invitation of John Raskob he became president of the newly organized Empire State, Inc., at a salary of $50,000 a year. There was, as yet, no Empire State Building except in the minds of Raskob and his associates, the DuPonts, and on the blueprints of their architects. The old Waldorf-Astoria, one of the world's most famous hotels, was on the site where the building one day would rise against the sky, and the demolition of that historic pile was not yet begun. Indeed, for publicity purposes, the day the wrecking crew went to work, Al sawed a cornice by way of touching off the operation.

"The first summons I ever served, back in the days when I was working in the office of the Commissioner of Jurors, was on a man who lived in this hotel," he said. "Little did I dream that there would be a day when I would be helping to tear the old building down."

His offices were at 331 Madison Avenue, although he shortly was to move to 200 Madison, which is at Thirty-sixth Street, where from his window he might watch the Waldorf being demolished and the new building rising in its place.

"Have you picked out a secretary yet?" Mrs. Moskowitz asked.

"No," he said.

"Well, I have one for you: Mary Carr."

"Great. Tell her to come to work here tomorrow."

The next thing was to get a place to live, for pleasant as life had been for the Smiths at the Biltmore, they wanted an apartment of their own. They had spent most of the summer at Hampton Bays, where Al derived a great deal of pleasure from swimming and from fishing for flounders, and now were ready to settle down in new surroundings in town. They signed a five-year lease on a penthouse apartment at 51 Fifth Avenue, near Washington Square.

He and Mrs. Smith had entered upon one of the happiest periods of their life together, and their apartment was the scene of family parties that the younger Smiths and their children never would forget. Kenny gave Al a hurdy-gurdy— for the children, he said, but of course Al got as much pleasure out of it as they did—and the children danced to its music as their parents and grandparents once had done on the sidewalks of Oliver Street.

As part of his daily routine, Al called Emily at her home in Albany, just to be sure that she and her husband and Mary, and little Emily, born in May of 1930, were well. And when any of his other children were out of town—or if he were out of town—he called them, too, every day. The Smith girls and boys were used to this, of course, but it never failed to impress those who had married into the family.

"I can't get over it," Major Warner once said. "In our family we used the telephone only in emergencies. This family uses it all the time."

And for the amusement of all, including Al, he would repeat the typical conversation he would overhear, or at least Emily's part of it:

" 'Hello, Father. How's Mother? That's good. Oh, we're all fine, thanks. Yes, really. Is Mother there? Put her on.... Hello, Mother. How's Father? That's good. Oh, we're all fine. Yes, really. Hello. Is that you, Father? All right. I'll hear from you tomorrow. Good-by.' "

When Emily was having her second baby, Al had gone to Albany and sat around for two weeks awaiting the big day. Then, having seen little Emily and made sure she and her mother were all right, he went back to New York and resumed his duties.

At one time he had stopped eating lunch, thinking in that way to recapture the slim waist line he had known as a youth, but his doctor told him that was not good for him and he never would get the waist line back anyway. Now luncheons became a part of his social life. Among his regular companions were John Raskob, Bill Kenny, Jim Ward, John Coleman, Orie Kelly, Gene Garey, Terence McManus, Dan Mooney, John Burke, John Smith, and George Van Namee— bankers, big businessmen, lawyers. Still nominally the first Democrat of of the land, he continued to take a keen interest in political affairs and was active in the councils of Tammany Hall, yet the average New Yorker, seeing the familiar brown derby on Fifth Avenue, already was beginning to look upon him more as a businessman than as a politician.

In May of 1931 the Empire State Building was opened and he moved into his office on the thirty-second floor. His high-backed chair was that he had had as governor. A side table was given over wholly to pictures of his family. The walls of his office and that of Mary Carr were covered with photographs and the originals of cartoons of him. The outer office where sat Detective Bill Roy, who had been his bodyguard for years, and had resigned from the Police Department to remain with him, was adorned with sketches of the Governor sent to him by amateur artists among his admirers. Some of them were exceptionally good and others were on the atrocious side, but he framed and hung every one of them.

The world's tallest building attracted thousands of sightseers daily, including famous men and women of all countries, and it seemed that all of them, the unknowns and the famous, considered him to be a part of the show. Had he met all those who wished to see him, he would have had no time in which to do his work, and Bill Roy and Mary Carr were hard pressed, sometimes, to keep the crowds at bay. But he saw as many of them as he could, and the impromptu receptions he sometimes held on the observation floor became little mob scenes.

One day, when Bill was away from his desk, a stranger

Al Smith, Cardinal Pacelli (now Pope Pius XII) and Mgr. Fulton J. Sheen in Rome, 1937

The Smith Family Gathers on Al's Seventieth Birthday

walked in and said that he would like to see the Governor before leaving for his home in Texas that afternoon. Mary, knowing that Al was busy going over some reports, said she was sorry but the Governor could not be disturbed; but the man hung on, talking glibly about his huge ranch in Texas, in which he knew the Governor would be interested, and mentioned something about sending the Governor some pheasants when he got home. That did it. Mary didn't want to cheat the Governor of a chance to get the pheasants.

"As I told you," she said, "the Governor is very busy, but I'll ask him if he can't see you for a few minutes, since you're leaving today."

The Governor, of course, would see anybody that had been passed upon by Mary, and the Texan was ushered in. Mary overheard him go into his patter about his ranch and the pheasants and then, to her dismay, for she knew what was coming, he said:

"Just before I came up to your office, I was in a department store in the neighborhood and my pocket was picked of four hundred and fifty dollars. I have my tickets home, of course, but I have only a few dollars left and I wondered—"

Bill had just returned to his desk and Mary said to him:

"Bill, I've done an awful thing. I let a man in to see the Governor and he is making a touch."

Bill peered into the office.

"Why, that bum!" he said. "I've chased him out of here a half dozen times in the last week!"

Just then the stranger came out, smiling. He bid Mary a cheery good-by, grinned at Bill, and sauntered toward the elevators.

Mary rushed into Al's office.

"I'm terribly sorry, Governor," she said. "I had no idea—"

"That's all right," he said, laughing. "I got off cheap. He was satisfied with a ten-dollar bill I offered him. Besides, I'm sure he's all right and that he'll send the ten back. And don't forget, he's going to send me some pheasants."

But the ten dollars never came back, nor were there any pheasants, although Al trustfully looked for them every day for a long while. When he finally became convinced that he had been duped, he said to Mary:

"Promise me you'll never tell the children about this. They'd kid the life out of me."

She never did.

33: END OF A POLITICAL CAREER

THERE ARE MANY WHO STILL BELIEVE THAT
Smith would have been nominated for the presidency
in 1932 if he had sought the nomination early enough—and
that if he had been nominated, he would have been elected.
This, of course, is purely conjectural and therefore mainly
of interest to students of what might have been.

All that anyone knows for certain is that he was hesitant
about offering himself as a candidate. Although defeated in
1928, he still loomed as the country's outstanding Democrat
as another presidential year rolled up, but when the question
of his running again first was raised he answered it with a
vigorous:

"What do you think I am? Another William Jennings
Bryan?"

This was good for a laugh—Bryan had tried three times to
be President and had been soundly beaten each time—but
it also gave heart to other aspirants for the designation.
Smith's supporters could not be turned aside so easily, however, and persisted in nudging him into the race, and he
finally agreed to enter it; but as he discovered at the Chicago
convention, he had got to the mark too late. By that time
James A. Farley had rounded up all the delegates that Franklin Roosevelt needed. Al, realizing he couldn't win, tried to
fend off the nomination of Roosevelt and failed there, too—
largely, he thought, because he was doublecrossed by William
G. McAdoo.

Disappointed on both counts, he announced that he was
"taking a walk," the inference being that he had turned his

back on his party and would not support its candidate in the campaign. This, it developed, wasn't so, but the possibility that it was frightened Roosevelt's adherents and, for a time, threatened to make a breach in the party lines through which the Republicans would march to another victory.

So far as he was concerned, the Chicago convention was written off with a laugh, provided by a dinner at the Empire State Club on July 20, when he gathered with those who had been closest to him through that losing engagement. The program of that dinner, which has become a collector's item, bears a picture of him on the cover and the inscription:

ALFRED E. SMITH

THE MAN WITH A RECORD WHO HAD A PROGRAM
MORAL VICTOR OF THE BATTLE OF CHICAGO, 1932
FIRST AND ONLY REUNION OF THE STAFF OF THE ALFRED E. SMITH
HEADQUARTERS, CONGRESS HOTEL, CHICAGO, 1932.

> *Politics is a thieves' game.*
> *Those who stay in it long enough*
> *are invariably robbed.*
> SHAKESPEARE.

The keynote of the dinner is to be found in the menu:

SUPREME OF MELON A LA CONGRESS
CELERY FARLEY   BRANCHLESS OLIVE ROOSEVELT   NUTS MCADOO
RAVIOLI NAPOLITAINE A LA SMITH
ROAST BONED MICHIGAN BOULEVARD SQUAB
(ONE IN EVERY POT)
CORN SAUTÉ
(COURTESY FEDERAL FARM BOARD)   SALADE DE SAISON POLITIQUE
COUPE EMPIRE STATE WITH MORTGAGE
(NO DEFICIT)
CAFÉ À LA STADIUM   TEA BISHOP CANNON

No one who was present at the dinner—and all the little group of those always faithful to him were there, Charlie Hand, Joe Cohn, the Moskowitzes, the Proskauers, Bob

Moses, and Mary Carr—and the others—ever will forget it. Al never was in better form, doubling as master of ceremonies and chief entertainer, singing, dancing, and making impromptu speeches that, unfortunately, never were recorded.

The almost frantic efforts of the national committee to get him behind Roosevelt were going on at this time—and he allowed them to go on for a while. Ultimately he caused the committee to give off a great sigh of relief by announcing that he not only desired the election of Roosevelt but would take the stump for him. A speech that he made in Boston, where he was tremendously popular, was one of the most effective blows struck in the entire campaign, and from Boston he went to Albany, where a reconciliation between him and Roosevelt had been arranged.

Roosevelt was at his desk in the Capitol when Al walked in. The atmosphere was strained, for even those who had brought the men together could not be sure how the meeting would come off; but whatever fears they nurtured were groundless. Al, smiling broadly, greeted Roosevelt with a hearty:

"Hello, you old potato!"

Roosevelt beamed happily as he clasped Smith's hand. So did everyone else in the room. The story of the meeting made pleasant reading for Democrats all over the country who, even after the Boston speech, still had been apprehensive. They felt that their troubles were over, as indeed they were. Roosevelt, going before the country under conditions vastly more favorable to the Democratic cause than Smith had found in 1928, was elected. It was because conditions had changed so sharply that Smith's friends felt that if he had been in Roosevelt's place, he would have won, too. Right or wrong, they felt that in 1928 he had laid the groundwork for the triumph in 1932. What he felt about it no one ever will know, simply because he never said anything about it, even to his closest friends.

The new governor of New York, elected as Roosevelt moved

up to the White House, was Herbert H. Lehman, banker, philanthropist, and public-spirited citizen, who had served as lieutenant-governor under Roosevelt and whom Smith had heartily endorsed as the head of the ticket in 1932. Al went to Albany for the inauguration on the first of January, 1933, and remaining over for a few days, was recalled hurriedly to New York by the tragic news that Mrs. Moskowitz had died.

She had been ill for a month as a result of a fall down the front steps of her home on West Ninety-fourth Street, but her family and friends had been hopeful that she soon would be up and about again. However, complications had developed and now she was dead.

Al was met at the Grand Central by newspapermen, who asked him if he cared to say anything about her and the part she had played in his political life. There were tears in his eyes and he found it difficult to speak. He shook his head. And then:

"She had the greatest brain of anybody I ever knew."

Although, as set forth earlier, stories of her influence over him had been exaggerated, sometimes in ignorance, sometimes in malice, Mrs. Moskowitz obviously had been the one on whom he had relied chiefly for assistance and advice. It had been a momentous day in the lives of both when Abram Elkus had asked her to work for Smith in the 1918 gubernatorial campaign, and the results achieved by their combined efforts had been of great and lasting value to the people of the state of New York. For all the good works she had done, Belle Moskowitz would be sorely missed, and by none more than by Al Smith.

In June of 1933 New York was getting ready, a long way in advance, for a mayoralty election. Jimmy Walker had resigned the year before and Fiorello H. LaGuardia, whom Jimmy once had defeated, was striking back. Running on a Fusion ticket, he surely would be elected unless—

Well, it was pretty obvious to the sachems at Tammany Hall: unless Al Smith could be induced to run on the Democratic ticket. They set their plans in motion, and word of what they had in mind reached LaGuardia. With typical candor, he said:

"It looks as though I have frightened them. They know I can beat anybody but Smith."

Everybody knew he was speaking the truth, and his election was virtually assured when Smith resolutely refused to accept the nomination. Had Al taken it, all party lines would have been shattered at the ballot booths in November, for never has there been a candidate for any office who exerted the sentimental pull that he would have had in running for mayor. It would have been, in the minds of all the voters of whatever party, the perfect arrangement to have this man, who had sprung to greatness from the sidewalks of New York, presiding in the City Hall. Only he could prevent his election, and he did so most effectively. The plan was to offer the nomination to him at the annual Fourth of July celebration at Tammany Hall. That day he went flounder fishing at Hampton Bays, leaving word that he was not to be disturbed, no matter who tried to get him on the telephone. The telephone rang . . . and rang . . . and members of the family answered it, but even when he came back from his fishing expedition and it continued to ring, he would not go near it.

He definitely was through with politics, so far as public office for himself was concerned. He always would be interested, naturally, in the affairs of his party, and he would be outspoken in praise or chastisement of one candidate or another, deeming that to be his duty as a citizen; and party loyalty would not curb his criticism, public or private, of Roosevelt in the time that remained to him. But never again would he offer himself, or allow himself to be drafted, to run for office.

ROM THERE ON HIS LIFE FOLLOWED A NEW
pattern. It had been sharply divided and marked out
by election years. For the Assembly... for sheriff... for
aldermanic president... for governor... for the presidency
of the United States. Now the years were fluid... and
merged... and his family and friends, speaking of them in
retrospect, frequently fumble for dates. They say:

"I do not remember what year it was, but I remember ..."

One day he was wanted at the Beekman Street Hospital:
two wealthy old ladies were about to make a tour of the hospital, with a view to contributing to its support, and no one
could be as charming as he toward prospective donors.

The first place he took the old ladies, who, regardless of
their good intentions, were on the prim side, was to the accident ward. In the first bed was a man with a badly shattered
leg.

"What happened to you?" Al asked.

The man looked up. His face lighted.

"Hello, Al!" he said. "How have you been? You don't
remember me, do you?"

"To tell you the truth, I don't. But your face is familiar."

The man laughed.

"It should be," he said. "A long time ago I was the bartender at Number Nine Bowery."

Al turned to the old ladies.

"I should have taken you to the children's ward," he said.

There was a big fight being held one night at the Polo
Grounds, and Bill Kenny and some of his other friends who

were going to the fight had dinner in the Tiger Room. Al joined them at dinner, but when it came time for them to start for the ringside, he refused to go with them.

"Who would go all the way up there on a hot night like this to see one man punch another on the nose?" he asked.

"We would," they said.

"You're crazy," he said.

He was, somehow, inveigled into going to a Notre Dame–Army football game.

"What did you think of it, Governor?" somebody asked.

"There is no sense to it," he said. "It looked to me as though there were twenty-two fellows out there trying to choke each other."

He attended a Giant opening for the purpose of throwing out the first ball, and then wished he hadn't because he had to sit through nine innings of a game that didn't interest him, when he could have been enjoying himself somewhere else.

Winston Churchill was in New York and after he and Al had dined together one night, Al said he wanted to attend a meeting of the district leaders at Tammany Hall and invited Churchill to go with him. After the meeting, he was curious to know what Churchill had thought of it.

"I was disappointed," Churchill said.

"Disappointed? Why?"

"There was no excitement. No matter what the man on the platform said, no one asked any questions."

"In Tammany Hall," Al said, "it is not considered good form to ask questions."

Then he told Churchill of the night Tom O'Brien tried to ask him a question.

There was a party at the Empire State Club one night for some distinguished musicians. A newspaper photographer was about to take a picture of the gathering when Al said:

"Wait a minute. There's a fellow back there who should be in the picture."

The fellow was backward about joining the group but Al insisted upon it.

"Who is he, Governor?" a reporter asked.

"William Brodie," Al said. "He played the piano in Tony Pastor's."

Walter's daughter, Catherine, then six years old, went to St. Vincent's Hospital to have her appendix removed. She wasn't seriously ill at the time, but her appendix had been giving her a lot of trouble and Dr. Raymond J. Sullivan, the family physician, thought it should come out. Naturally, she was fearful at mention of the hospital.

"There's nothing to worry about," Al said. "I'll go with you. In fact, I will be right in the next room."

When they reached the hospital in the evening, Catherine was put to bed and he sat beside her until she fell asleep.

While she was being operated on, the following day, Al sat by a telephone in his apartment, anxiously awaiting word from Dr. Sullivan. On each of the other telephones in the apartment was hung a sign: "Important! Do not use this telephone!" Not until Dr. Sullivan had called to say that Catherine had come safely through the operation was anyone in the family allowed to use one of the other telephones. Al was afraid the Doctor might get his numbers mixed.

At Christmastime, all the grandchildren were instructed that their letters to Santa Claus must be mailed to the Empire State Building in care of their grandfather. He would copy off the lists of the toys they wanted and do all the shopping himself. The presents were sent to his office, where he and Mary Carr would check them against the lists, after which they would be wrapped and delivered. This was followed by a check with their parents. He thought it would be tragic if even one of the toys asked for should be missing on Christmas morning. The little Smiths, Warners, and Quillinans thought Santa Claus was wonderful.

When gas rationing went into effect, he wanted to know how much gas he could get on any A ticket. Learning that it wasn't enough to take him to see the Warners at Southampton or the Quillinans at Rye, he said he would dispose of his two cars.

"Why don't you ask for a B ticket?" his friends asked.

"I'm not entitled to it," he said.

"You do a lot of traveling about in your charitable work."

"Well, I can take a cab, can't I?"

One of his cars happened to be in the Quillinan's garage.

"Sell it," he said to Catherine. "I'm going to sell the other one, too. I'll get a job for John."

John was his chauffeur.

Shortly after that, he made a radio appeal for the sale of war bonds. As a feature of the sale, it was announced that anyone who bought a bond over the telephone might speak to him. After the broadcast, he was in the telephone room answering the calls that flooded the switchboard. He heard one of the operators say:

"How do you spell it, Miss? Q-u-i-l-l—"

He motioned for her to let him have the call. When he was connected, he said:

"Where did you get the money to buy a bond?"

Catherine, on the other end of the wire, laughed and said:

"That was my commission for selling your car."

When it became difficult to get a cab outside the Empire State Building to take him home, he began to use the Fifth Avenue buses. He liked them so well that he used them regularly. One night, when it was raining hard, the driver of his bus pulled up in front of his home, now at 820 Fifth Avenue, so that all he had to do was to step from the bus and he was under the canopy. All the other passengers cheered.

His new home was at Sixty-third Street, which—an added attraction for him—was handy to the Central Park Zoo. He was made the Honorary Night Superintendent of the Zoo and it became his habit, after dinner nearly every night, to visit the animals and make sure they were all right.

"I've got a new girl friend," he boasted. "She lives right near me. Her name is Rosie."

Rosie was a hippopotamus.

Mrs. Dan Mooney was ill in Medical Center, away uptown at One Hundred and Sixty-eighth Street. He was going up to see her late one afternoon, bearing a huge box of flowers, and although it had been a rather trying day for him at the office, he decided, for some reason, to take the subway. Mary Carr and Bill Roy sought to dissuade him, but it was no use. Bill, worried that he might get lost, walked to the subway station with him and saw him safely on a train. The rush hour had just begun and the train was crowded. The next morning Mary asked him how he had fared.

"Very nicely," he said. "I was holding on to the flowers with one hand and a rail with the other and a young girl took pity on me and gave me her seat."

"Do you think she recognized you?"

"No. I don't think she did."

But if the girl in the subway didn't recognize him, thousands of other persons did as he walked on the avenues or rode the buses. It was his custom to have lunch with Jim Ward and John Coleman and George Van Namee and some of his other friends at the Manhattan Club on Saturdays (when he wasn't attending the meetings of the Occasional Thinkers with Nicholas Murray Butler), and after lunch they would walk up to the Biltmore.

Always, on these walks, men would stop him.

"Do you remember me, Governor? I met you in Atlantic City with Charlie Murphy...."

"How do you do, Governor? The last time I saw you was in Boston the night..."

And each was made to feel that, sure, the Governor remembered him.

Others simply would turn to look at him, pointing him out to their companions. One day Jim Ward, walking with him, said jokingly:

"It is possible these people know who you are?"

"No," he said. "They just admire the way I wear my clothes. I'm the mold of fashion and the glass of form."

When, during the week, he didn't lunch at the Empire State Club, he would take Bill Roy to a near-by Childs restaurant where, without fail, he ordered ham and beans.

"For him too," he would say, indicating Bill.

Bill would grumble, but to no avail. Ham and beans would make him big and strong, Al always said. And Bill, who was big and strong enough to tear the building down with his hands, would say:

"A guy might just as well be in the Navy."

Ham and beans... sauerbraten and potato cakes... Italian food of any kind... these were Al's favorite dishes. Luchow's, a German restaurant on Fourteenth Street, attracted him often for dinner. No one could cook sauerbraten as well as Luchow's chef, he said. No one, that is, but Arthur's wife, Anne.

His mail was terrific. That is the only word for it, bearing on both its volume and content. Most of it was serious, of course, but a daffy thread ran through it. Mash notes, for instance:

I saw you up in the Empire State Tower today. You were talking with two men making a record. I wanted to speak to you but

I was afraid you would think I was too fresh. So I kept looking at you and when you went to the lunch room, I came down.

I eat every Tuesday from 12 to 1 at —— restaurant. I would love to see you if you have a few minutes. Please come.

                                                                    Hope

A man in Indianapolis had a sure way to protect the Empire State Building from German bombs. The fact that in order to install his device it would be necessary to remove the roof didn't seem important tc him.

Begging letters were high on the list. One was from a woman in DePauw, Indiana, who obviously did not keep up with the news. It was addressed to "Mr. Smith, President of the Younited States, Washington, D.C."

A Kentuckian wrote:

I am the Hon. ——. I am the 7th wonder of the world. I want 500 without delay. Please send same at once. We are all O.K. I am 79 yr of age. I was born in 1855. I am the 7th son and the father of 7 children. I am a full blooded Irishmen.

And from Milwaukee:

This is unusual but I am in need. Would you send me $2500, as this is the amount I am in need of. I will give you as collateral my word of honor that I will repay you if possible. If not, let the good Lord repay you and he will also pay better interest. I will send you 3% yearly.

Not all the letters asking for financial aid were from screwballs. Especially during the depression, he received hundreds of appeals from men and women who simply were desperate. It saddened him because he could not help these people. Countless others wrote to him for jobs—and many of them were put to work in the Empire State Building.

A letter which interested him very much, principally because of the roundabout, storybook manner in which it reached him, was tossed from the S.S. *Manhattan* "five days and 1700 miles from New York." It was signed by four men who, apparently, had enjoyed the evening in the ship's smoking room one night in October of 1932 and it was filled with praise of him, and regret that he had not been nominated at Chicago. He received it in September of 1934, the bottle having been plucked from the sea by James Gleason of St. Kearns, Saltmills, County Wexford, Ireland, who wrote, in effect, that he, too, was a great admirer of his.

It was in this period of his life that Al became an enthusiastic amateur photographer (he really achieved some little skill with a camera once he learned to stop bending over so far and thus cutting off the heads of his adult subjects) and it delighted him to have some of his celebrated guests pose for him with Mrs. Smith. A number of these shots were treasured by him and he gave them an honored place next to the album of pictures he had taken of his grandchildren.

Little things, these ... but little pieces of a man's life. There were the bigger, more important things, the dates of which are well remembered.

In 1933 he received the Catholic Action Medal and honorary degrees from Harvard, Columbia, the University of the State of New York and St. Bonaventure's. That year, too, Cardinal Hayes asked him to form a committee of the laity to foster the spread of Catholic charities in New York, and he gladly consented to do so. This committee, composed, in the beginning, of his closest friends—John Coleman was one of his most active and devoted aides—grew through the years, raised great sums of money, and administered them wisely. As the Archbishop's Committee, named for Archbishop Spellman, following the death of Cardinal Hayes, it remains as a living memorial to its organizer.

In 1937 he made his first and only trip to Europe. He was accompanied by Mrs. Smith—who had been across once before, with John and Emily Warner—Mr. and Mrs. Mooney, Mr. and Mrs. Eugene Garey, and Mr. and Mrs. Richard Corroon. The little red-covered notebook he always carried, in which he jotted down his engagements, gives a brief outline of the tour: Rome . . . Florence . . . Milan . . . Avignon . . . Carcasonne . . . Lourdes . . . Paris . . . London . . . "Ireland at last!" There are few added notations. One, under London, is "Tea with Winston Churchill." Ignored were meetings with Mussolini in Rome, Chamberlain in London, and DeValera in Dublin.

Most curious of all is the omission of what, undeniably, was the greatest experience of his life: an audience with His Holiness, Pope Pius XI.

The following year he was elevated to the rank of Papal Chamberlain by the Pope in recognition of his charitable works in the Archdiocese of New York. Invested with him were two others, John S. Burke and John Thomas Smith, the ceremony taking place at the new Waldorf-Astoria, with Cardinal Hayes presiding. Those present were greatly impressed by the solemnity of the occasion, and when the newly created chamberlains were called upon to speak, following the Cardinal, Burke and John Smith, being shy men in any circumstances, scarcely could find words with which to express their feelings.

Al, with that composure which never deserted him, broke down an atmosphere that fast was becoming overwhelming. The work he had done in Catholic charities was nothing, he said. Certainly it had been no hardship. The only time he ever had borne hardship for the church was when he was an altar boy at St. James's and had to serve at the six o'clock mass on winter mornings. And as he told of those days, so long ago, his hearers could see him, trudging the dark length of Cherry Street, stopping to pick up a boy named Johnny Keating who served with him, and trudging on again. But it was no pathetic picture of himself that he painted. It was shot through with the rare humor that he could put into the telling of a story—and none appreciated it more than the Cardinal, who was born and reared just a little south by west of Al, in City Hall Place.

In 1939 he went to California again. This time the object was pleasure alone. The trip had its beginning in idle talk at his apartment one night. Orie Kelly and Dan Mooney and their wives were there, and the usual Alfred and Katie Smith Special Poker Game was in progress—a game such as never had been seen before or since: sixty cards instead of fifty-two. Cards that were marked as elevens and twelves. And deuces and eights wild. You played for three hours and spent the next two hours finding out how much you had won or lost, with chips valued at a cent. And after all that, you found that you had won . . . or lost . . . anywhere from a nickel to thirty-five cents or, if your run of luck had been extremely bad, you might have lost almost a dollar.

Between hands . . . because there was nothing especially grim about the game, except when Al, holding four twelves, would be betting as much as a quarter . . . the men were talking about needing a rest . . . and how about the six of them going on a trip somewhere? The more they discussed it, the better it sounded, and by the time the game broke up they had decided that as soon as they could arrange to do so, they would spend six weeks on a leisurely trip to the coast, stopping off where they pleased, going about and seeing things.

It was a wonderful trip, but not altogether in the way they had visioned. They went to all the places they had planned and saw all the things they had mapped out for themselves—but they hadn't taken into account the fact that, eleven years after he had stumped the country in quest of the presidency, Al Smith would be hailed as a national hero.

"I never saw anything like it," Kelly said, on his return. "Triumphant tours, with motorcycle escorts. Official receptions. Keys to the cities. Reporters. Photographers. It took Al completely by surprise, of course. But it did his heart—and our hearts—good to see that, in all the time that had passed since he last toured the country, the people had not forgotten."

35: "IT IS GOD'S WILL"

THE ROLLING YEARS, THE PLEASANT YEARS...
and then the somber years and a man growing old.
Seeing the shape of things to come and, putting aside personal differences with the President, supporting him in his
attempts to rouse the nation to its peril. The clash of war,
and young Al and John Warner in the armed forces ... and
the man throwing himself again into war work, as he had
done in 1917 ... and the years catching up with him and
his health failing. Going into the hospital in the early spring
of 1943—for a rest, they thought. And coming out and throwing himself once more into the tasks that crowded him fast.
Never complaining but trying hard to keep from his wife
and his family and his friends the fact that the years were
catching up with him.

He was not a well man in 1943. When pain racked him,
he said nothing, but the marks of his illness were beginning
to show in his face, and although there was no slackening of
the drive with which he attacked his work, Mrs. Smith and
his children and the others close to him looked at him
anxiously now and then.

The year whirled on ... and now it was December and on
the thirtieth he was seventy years old. Messages of congratu-
lation poured in upon him. Pope Pius XII who, as Cardinal
Pacelli, had become his friend, cabled his blessing. There
was a party for him at the Empire State Club, given by old
friends and new, including many of the Archbishop's Committee of the Laity.

In the evening, there was a family party at his apartment. It was the biggest family party the Smiths ever had, because every year there were more children in the family. It was not, in itself, a surprise. How could it be, when no member of the family ever had a birthday without a party? But there was a grand surprise in store for the Governor, even so. Young Al, still in this country at the time, was coming home and his father didn't know it. Only Emily knew it and she didn't tell anybody, even her mother. When he didn't arrive on schedule, Emily began to worry, fearing his leave suddenly had been canceled. She stalled off the photographer who had been engaged to take a picture of the party for the family. Stalled him as long as she could. When the others began demanding that the picture be taken so they could get on with the fun, she had to give in. They all took their places and the picture was made—and just then the door opened and young Al came tearing in. There was so much excitement and everybody made so much noise that the baby (Alfred E. Smith II, Walter's youngest son) burst into tears and it was some time before everybody was straightened out again and another picture was taken, this time with young Al in it.

January... February... March. It was a mild day and Al and Jim Ward were playing golf. They were talking of one thing and another and got into the wartime political situation and Jim said:

"I suppose if the war continues into the summer, Roosevelt will run for president again."

"Yes."

"Will you vote for him?"

"I'll be able to tell you better in the fall," Al said. Then: "If I'm here."

It was the first time he ever had said anything like that. Probably the only time. Ward didn't say anything, and Al went on talking about the political situation.

On the morning of April 1, Mrs. Smith, who had complained mildly of a cold in her chest, had a bad coughing spell. She plainly was suffering from something far more serious than a cold, and Al called Dr. Sullivan, who ordered her immediate removal to St. Vincent's. Al, suddenly alarmed about her, was almost distracted when, having seen her settled in the hospital, he hurried to his office, intending to clean up the work that awaited him and hurry back to the hospital.

He had forgotten, in his apprehension, that he had agreed to take part in the making of a motion picture to be made by the Army that morning as one of a series to be shipped to homesick New York soldiers overseas. When he arrived and saw officers and cameramen waiting for him, he looked startled, and after a word of greeting to them excused himself and went into an inner office. Mary Carr, who had been informed of Mrs. Smith's illness but did not realize the seriousness of it, was shocked to find him in tears. When he told her of his fears for his wife, she urged him to permit her to explain to the Army group and ask them to leave.

"No," he said. "I'll be all right in a few minutes."

He managed to control his grief, to go smiling through the part outlined for him in the picture. It was not until the last shot had been made that the director and cameramen knew of the strain under which he had worked with them.

Under treatment Mrs. Smith seemed to improve and there was a day when Al, coming from her bedside, was greatly relieved. In this reaction there was a nervous gaiety about him. He regaled Mary Carr and Bill Roy with stories of his boyhood that they had not heard before, acting some of them out, singing old songs, once or twice breaking into a dance, to show them how he had done it on some occasion in the long ago.

His happiness was short-lived. Mrs. Smith was not getting

well, he now believed. He stopped Dr. Thomas Martin, a heart specialist, outside her room one day.

"Doctor," he said, "I am going to ask you a direct question. All I want from you is 'Yes,' or 'No.' Is Mrs. Smith any better today than she was the day she entered the hospital?"

The doctor looked at him steadily.

"No," he said.

"Thank you, Doctor," Al said.

That was all. But now he knew. He knew that his wife was going to die. That the happy years, through which their love for each other had grown steadily, were drawing fast to an end. That there was no hope for her, nothing that he or the doctors or anyone else could do.

On May 4, as Al and her children gathered at her bedside, Mrs. Smith died.

Friends came swiftly to offer their condolences, and, strong in his faith in the midst of bereavement, he said to them:

"It was God's will that it should be so. God has been very good to us, giving us a long and happy life together and sparing her until her children were grown and had children of their own to add to her happiness. Hard as it is for me to part with her, I know there must be some reason why He has taken her."

Emily had closed the Warner home in Albany when the Major went overseas with the Army and she had moved into the Fifth Avenue apartment with her father and mother. She, with perhaps a keener insight than any other member of the family, had been sure for a long time that her father's condition was serious. Now, with her mother gone, she was her father's constant companion, as indeed she had been during her mother's illness. The other members of the family— young Al's wife, Walter and Arthur and their wives, and the Quillinans—were equally devoted to him. So, too, did his friends watch over him and, as his strength waned with the passing weeks, he never had a lonely evening, for there was always someone to dine with him at home or go out with him of an evening.

One night, at a meeting of the Archbishop's Committee, there was talk of the new motion picture, Bing Crosby's *Going My Way*. Al wasn't much interested at first and John Coleman said:

"You really should see it, Governor. You'd like it, I know."

He told him about Bing as the young priest, and the delightful characterization of an old and sometimes crotchety priest by Barry Fitzgerald, of the tough kids, especially the one who slapped another in the face, commanding him to "say hello to de Fadder."

"It sounds very good," Al said. "I think I'd like to see it."

A private showing was arranged for him and he invited a group of young priests to attend it with him. He enjoyed it immensely, now laughing, now watching with tears in his eyes, now laughing again as the story unfolded. When it was over, he said:

"It reminded me of the days when I was a boy at St. James's."

36: DEATH TAKES THE GOVERNOR

IT WAS JUNE AND THERE WAS A DAY IN THE office when Mary Carr became alarmed. There had been other days when Al had drowsed at his desk as a long afternoon wore on, but this day he had not gone through his morning's mail before he began to nod in his chair. At her own desk in the outer office, Mary could see him, reflected in the glasses of the picture frames on the wall...nodding... rousing himself...nodding again.

She called Francis Quillinan on the telephone.

"I think you'd better have Dr. Sullivan look in on the Governor tonight," she said. "He isn't a bit well today."

That night the doctor arrived at the apartment.

"I was in the neighborhood and thought I'd drop in and say hello," he said.

Al wasn't surprised to see him. The Doctor had been in the habit of dropping in lately. It was always by chance, Al thought.

"Hello," he said, smiling wanly.

"You look tired," the Doctor said.

"I am. I was dozing all day in the office."

"I'm not surprised to hear it. What you need is a rest. Why not let me put you in St. Vincent's for a few days?"

"In the hospital? What for? I'll have a good night's sleep right here and I'll be all right in the morning."

But the Doctor was quietly insistent, and in the end, Al allowed himself to be driven to the hospital.

He was back at his office in a few days, looking better and declaring that he never felt better in his life. But indeed he was a sick man, and although he had held up resolutely through Mrs. Smith's illness and death, he was failing rapidly now. Drowsiness would assail him, sometimes even in the midst of his dictation of a letter. He had severe headaches.

"Why don't you take an aspirin?" Mary would ask.

He would look at her as though she had suggested his taking poison.

"No," he would say.

He didn't believe in taking anything.

"Don't worry about me. I'll be all right."

He spent a couple of weeks with Emily in Southampton— he had insisted she take her children to their summer place for a vacation—and returned to his desk tanned and chipper. On July 25, which was Mary Warner's birthday, he went to Southampton again, accompanied this time by Arthur's two young sons. Emily had a party for her daughter and Al seemed himself again, singing the old songs, dancing a jig, waltzing with Emily and her daughters. But the next morning he scarcely touched his breakfast. That was a bad sign.

"You don't feel well," Emily said.

"No," he admitted, "I didn't sleep well last night."

He was going back to town shortly after breakfast.

"I'll go with you," Emily said. "I have some shopping to do in New York. I was going up tomorrow, but I'd rather ride up with you and the boys."

She had no shopping to do. She thought he might be taken ill on the way, and in that case she wanted to be with him. She left word that she would remain at the apartment that night, just to be sure he was all right or to care for him if he needed her.

She had thought, as they arrived in town, that her father would go directly to the apartment, but he said he was going to the office. He was determined to go there, so she did not argue with him.

When they reached the Empire State Building, he said to the boys:

"All right, young fellows. You can go home now."

And to Mary:

"Do your shopping and drop back here. We'll go uptown together."

He worked all afternoon and seemed better for it. He was in excellent spirits at dinner, retired early, and arose at seven in the morning as usual. His appetite was normal, meaning that he ate a huge breakfast. Greatly relieved, Emily went back to Southampton.

Friday, August 4, was an unusually hot day.

"You could have fried an egg on the sidewalk outside the Empire State Building," John Coleman said.

John called for Al to take him down to his summer home at Spring Lake, New Jersey.

"He looked wilted," John said, "but so did everybody else. I thought the week end at the shore would do him a lot of good."

On the way down, John almost regretted having taken him, for he looked very ill. But when they reached the house and Al got into a bathing suit and had a dip in the pool, he seemed much better. Saturday . . . Sunday . . . he did rather well. Monday morning he looked bad again and seemed more than a little worried.

"This fresh air is all right," he said, smiling thinly, "but what I need to fix me up is a steaming hot bath at the Biltmore."

The sun had failed to make him perspire freely. What he needed was to be boiled out. Then he would feel all right.

Coleman decided not to take the early morning train to the city and his office. He would wait and ride up with Al, just to be sure.

Back in town, Al went to the baths. He asked Coleman if he didn't want to go with him.

"No thanks," John said, laughing. "When I want to get into a hot tub, I'll do it at home. I'll call you later."

When he called, Al said he felt fine. He didn't sound it. John was concerned.

"You'd better take it easy," he said.

The next morning, the Governor was unable to leave his bed. Toward evening, the doctor was worried. He called Emily.

"Come up to town," he said. "I'm taking your father to the hospital."

She rushed for a train and barely missed it. The next train didn't reach New York until after eleven o'clock, too late for her to see her father that night. The next morning she walked into his room just as he awakened. Without turning his head and thinking it was a nurse who had entered the room, he said:

"Will you please call my daughter, Mrs. Warner, at Southampton, and tell her I'd like her to come to see me?"

"I don't think that will be necessary," she said.

He turned quickly and, smiling, he said:

"I really didn't think it would be."

He seemed to gain strength the first few days in the hospital. He began to worry about his correspondence piling up in his office ... about checks to be signed.

"Tell Mary when she comes tomorrow to bring those checks with her," he said to Emily one night.

Mary Carr had been to see him every day, but there had been no mention of his business affairs, of course.

"What checks?" Emily asked.

"Mary will know," he said.

In the night he suffered a relapse. When Mary arrived in the morning he was lying very flat and he was very white, and Mary, who had brought the checks, said nothing about them to him but sat at his bedside with Emily for a short time and went back to the office.

On September 22, which was a Friday, he was removed to the Rockefeller Institute, where he picked up again. His voice, which had failed him, returned. When Mary Carr visited him on September 30, he said:

"The bills for the apartment will be coming in tomorrow. Get the money and pay them."

"All right," she said. "I'll take care of them."

"I know you will," he said. "But I was just thinking about them and I thought I would remind you."

That night he took a sudden turn for the worse. Emily was frightened and sent for his old friend, Father John Healy, who anointed him. The next morning he seemed a little better. His mind was clear, his voice strong again. Father Healy called, and he and Emily sat at the bedside. After a time, thinking her father had dropped off into sleep, Emily left the room. When she had gone, Al opened his eyes and looked steadily at the priest.

"Am I dying, Father?" he asked.

"Yes," the priest said.

There was no change of expression on the patient's face. "Start the Act of Contrition," he said.

That night the Most Reverend Francis A. McIntyre, Auxiliary Bishop of New York, visited him. He was very low and the Bishop administered the last rites of the church to him. Shortly afterward he became unconscious. Early in the morning of Friday, October 4, he died.

On October 6, as he lay in state in St. Patrick's Cathedral the police estimated that more than 160,000 persons filed past his bier. They came from everywhere. From all sides of the town. From all its social strata. And in the crowd, walking silently through the great cathedral, could be heard, softly, the heartbeat of the city he loved.

193

195 - 196

197

204 - 205 206

211

215

100

18

80

8

159

155

152

182

182

75

98

122

246

122